BRITNEY

Breaking Free

Also by Danny White

Adele

Harry

Ariana

Rihanna

BRITNEY
Breaking Free

THE UNAUTHORIZED BIOGRAPHY

Danny White

Michael O'Mara Books Limited

First published in Great Britain in 2022 by
Michael O'Mara Books Limited
9 Lion Yard
Tremadoc Road
London SW4 7NQ

A CIP catalogue record for this book is available from the British Library.

This product is made of material from well-managed, FSC®-certified forests
and other controlled sources. The manufacturing processes conform to the
environmental regulations of the country of origin.

ISBN: 978-1-78929-459-0 in hardback print format
ISBN: 978-1-78929-479-8 in trade paperback format
ISBN: 978-1-78929-461-3 in ebook format

1 2 3 4 5 6 7 8 9 10

Cover design by Natasha Le Coultre
Designed and typeset by D23
Front cover photography: WENN Rights Ltd/Alamy Stock Photo
Back cover photography: © Mjt/AdMedia via ZUMA Wire/Alamy Stock Photo
Printed and bound by CPI Group (UK) Ltd, Croydon, CR0 4YY

www.mombooks.com

CONTENTS

INTRODUCTION

When Britney Spears was dramatically released from her conservatorship in 2021, the reporters massed outside the court asked her attorney when the world could expect new music from the pop idol. With his four-word reply, he summed up perfectly the new reality the court had just handed his client. 'It's up to her,' he said.

She had waited so long to be back in charge of her own destiny, but for many the burning question is not what Britney will do after her conservatorship, but what happened before and during it. In front of our very eyes, this sassy, feisty pop icon was put under such harsh restrictions that her father even had the final say over what colour cabinets she had in her kitchen and she was forced into a mental health facility against her will. She even had to justify every cup of coffee she bought. It was a highly controlling arrangement, compared by Britney herself to 'sex trafficking'. How did it come to this, and what were the demons that led to her very public downward spiral?

Britney has long been an artist of contradictions and mixed messages. In her very first auditions as a pop hopeful, record label bosses were bewitched by what was then her curious blend of wholesome, southern Christian girl and doe-eyed nymph. In the first song they gave her, she sang the lyrics 'Hit me, baby' and danced suggestively in a school uniform in the promotional video. Her first major magazine cover saw her pose erotically in bed while surrounded by childhood paraphernalia. She was just eighteen.

For years, she insisted in interviews that she was a virgin, even as her songs and videos continued to deliberately tease the world. She wanted to have it both ways, and this captivated the public. But there is a price for playing those games. Britney became exhausted by the media's obsession about whether she was still a virgin. She found questions about her body and her sex life intrusive and took her split from Justin Timberlake very badly when the media tried to paint her as the villain. As far back as 2002, the fun went out of the game for Britney. It was as if the lights in her eyes had been switched off, and before long she was on the path to meltdown in full view of the world's tabloid media.

She spontaneously married in Las Vegas after a mammoth drinking session, divorcing just fifty-five hours later as her family and management panicked that her sudden spouse might get access to her fortune. She shaved her hair off in front of media cameras and attacked a photographer's car with an umbrella. She was in and out of rehab. For her parents, who had both witnessed tragedy first-hand as children, this behaviour was extremely alarming. They became terrified about some of the people around Britney and also feared for the safety of their grandchildren.

During the conservatorship years, another contradiction formed which never quite sat right with her fans. Britney seemed to be the hardest working woman in pop. She was forever recording, performing and promoting. She did a residency in Las Vegas. She presented herself to the world as stable and industrious. Yet her guardians continued to argue that she was in a position of such vulnerability that they had to control every fibre of her existence.

We all feel we know Britney Spears. Older pop fans have watched her grow up since she emerged onto the scene in 1998, while younger fans have never known a world without her. She has sold over 150 million records and commanded relentless attention from the media. We've seen her at her heights, performing imperiously on the biggest stages, and we've seen her lows, as she was strapped down and taken to a mental health facility.

As the princess of pop, she has seen other acts come and go. Britney released her first single in 1998. That year, she shared the charts with the likes of Boyzone, All Saints and Aqua, all long since forgotten. None of the stars she shares the spotlight with now were active when Britney began: Adele was ten years old, Harry Styles was just four and Billie Eilish hadn't even been born. Yet Britney's music continues to be part of the soundtrack to our lives and she continues to be a source of fascination for the media.

She feels like one of the family to millions, but how well do we really know her? Such is the longevity, scale and success of her career and the tragedies of her story that rather than compare her to any of today's more short-lived pop stars, it's more helpful to compare her to the likes of Marilyn Monroe and Princess Diana. Like those two figures, she has come to represent much more than what initially made her famous. Instead, she symbolizes the pressures that fame puts upon female celebrities in particular'.

However much scandal, tragedy and adversity haunts her, Britney always manages to keep going. Despite being in the most unforgiving and fickle industry of all, she is now in her third decade at the top. Many divas have spoken and sung of being survivors, but Britney has survived right in front of our eyes.

Yet it is only when you go behind the scenes that you can understand how she has managed this. So, who is the real Britney Spears? What is the truth behind the infamous tabloid headlines? And how did she end up entering – and then leaving – her conservatorship? In telling her life story, this book is an attempt to answer those questions.

Chapter One

A GIRL IN A HURRY

She was featured in a newspaper when she was eight weeks old. She took her first dance class at the age of two. She made her public singing debut when she was four. At five, she sang for hours in the bathroom, to an audience of teddy bears and dolls. She entered her first talent contest at the age of six. She was a girl in a hurry.

Britney Jean Spears was born on 2 December 1981 and baptized as a Southern Baptist. Her mother, Lynne, was the daughter of a dairy farmer and worked as a day-care supervisor. She had met Britney's father, Jamie, at high school and was just twenty-one when they married. Their first year of marriage was 'really quite idyllic', wrote Lynne in the memoir she co-wrote with Britney, *Heart to Heart*. They lived in Florida for a few months and were able to build up a nest egg. However, it was not the smoothest of love stories. Although Lynne had declared her love for Jamie when they got married, looking back she realized that it was only during the first year of their marriage that she actually fell in love with him.

Then, she fell pregnant. She and Jamie were so excited. He waited on her hand and foot as they waited for the birth and she craved all sorts of foods, including ice cream,

Snickers bars, fried chicken, pears and cottage cheese. Just nine months after they had wed, they had their first child, a son called Bryan. Lynne remembered worrying that the locals would gossip about the birth coming so soon after the wedding, but Bryan was 'about as all-boy as you can get', said Lynne. It felt great to be a mother.

Soon after, Britney came along. Lynne was in labour for twenty-one hours, but she doesn't hold it against her daughter. She was just delighted it had all gone safely. The family lived in Kentwood, Louisiana, which was a small town – or, a 'small, small town', said Britney – based on farming, in the 1980s. Jamie worked in construction, but during Britney's childhood that sort of work became harder to come by, forcing him to travel further afield in pursuit of the dollar.

Kentwood was not much of a place, but it was home. Lynne wrote that it was 'not exactly an exotic destination', adding, 'There's basically the Kentwood Café, Connie's Jewellers, a bunch of dollar stores,' with a Sonic Drive-In proving 'the hub of the community'.

Her daughter, Jamie Lynn, wrote later that everyone says good morning to each other and everyone knows each other's names. 'It's the type of place where everyone knows each other's business,' she added in her memoir *Things I Should Have Said*. As of 2022, it had a population of just 2,448. Britney remains its most famous child.

Jamie and Lynne did their best to provide a comfortable home for Britney to grow up in. The living room, with its beige carpet and blue sofa, included a family piano for

Britney to sing at and enough room for her to dance around, including the backflips she loved.

At the age of 'about two', remembered Lynne, Britney took dance classes at the Renee Donewar School of Dance in Kentwood. The proud mum remembers how Britney would take the lead and marshal the kids, most of whom were little more than babies, looking helplessly cute, dolled up in tutus and ballet shoes.

Lynne recalled how thrilled she was to have an 'adorable baby girl to dress up like a little doll', in words that unwittingly presaged the objectification that her daughter would experience as a celebrity. Stardom was a destiny that Britney showed signs of from the start. Lynne remembered that when her daughter was 'only a year or two old' she would already have her 'hands on her hips, lips pouting' for the camera. An incalculable number of photographs would be taken of her daughter in the future.

Her family believes that Britney's musical talent comes from her mother's side of the family. Her great-aunt, Joan Woolmore, told the *Daily Mail* that although she and Britney's grandmother, Lilian, came from 'humble beginnings', they loved to 'dance and play music'. She recalled how their father would save up so he could send them to dance classes and piano lessons. They went to classes at the Royal Opera House in Covent Garden. 'We could jitterbug with the best of them,' she said.

During a visit to England, Lynne met her aunt Joan and uncle Archie for the first time. 'I remember being full of admiration for the British way of life,' she wrote in *Heart to*

Heart. 'Sitting in the Woolmore garden, having tea with my relatives, I gathered that the English valued education and travel, and they felt travel was indeed an integral part of one's education.' This love of Britain seemed to have an air of nominative determinism for ... Britney.

Meanwhile, back at home Britney's bedroom was small and cluttered, not least with dolls and teddy bears. She would move her collection to the bathroom and sing and dance for them. However, they were not the focus of her attention. The large mirror would allow her to gaze intently at herself as she performed. As she stood on the edge of the bath tub, she was fascinated by how she looked. Britney was her own first fan. She would practise smiling and blowing kisses to future audiences.

For Britney's weekly dance classes, Lynne would drive her 30 miles to the town of Hammond, where teacher Renee Donewar taught her and other little girls ballet. Britney was not just along for the ride; she took the classes very seriously. She always learned new steps fastest, won the best attendance prize and had little tolerance for any classmates who did not try as hard as her. Many critics have remarked over the years that Britney is a better dancer than singer. Whatever the truth of that, it was here that she started to hone her moves, and it was also where she first showed her extraordinary and exacting dedication.

Then, when she was four, Britney was singled out for her talents for the first time when her dance tutor asked her to perform a solo dance at a recital. 'I just stepped back and watched, proud, of course, but also somewhat puzzled as to where she got those natural gifts as a dancer,' wrote her mother. Nevertheless, she was thrilled to be able to support her 'Brit' in her hobby. Lynne has written that 'there is no greater joy than finding your meaning in life – except maybe helping someone you love find hers'. She tried her best to perform exactly this role for Britney, helping her chase her passion for music.

Britney was also a sporty girl who enjoyed summer evenings playing basketball. She played point guard for the school team, with the number twenty-five shirt on her back. 'I loved it,' she said in *Heart to Heart*. 'I could play basketball all night long, but would have to be up in the morning to help out at Granny's deli.' She was also a dedicated gymnast who would spend an average of five evenings a week in the gym.

She continued the movements at home, practising those backflips and other moves with the help of a balance beam her father had installed for her. She joined local competitions and then took her hobby further afield, travelling to a camp run by Olympic coach Béla Károlyi. He remembered her as 'one of the little girls who excelled', but Britney ultimately found that the higher up the gymnastics ladder she climbed, the less fun there was to be had.

She told Lynne that it was becoming too hard for her and she wanted to give up on gymnastics to focus more on dance. Lynne had started to have doubts herself. She had spotted girls weighing themselves after classes and freaking out if they were just one pound overweight. Lynne worried for a while that she should not agree to Britney's request to stop doing gymnastics. However, she believed that you must trust your child's instincts.

Lynne and Britney were becoming closer and closer as a result of these conversations. Other relatives noticed how tight a unit and how similar mother and daughter were. 'Sometimes Britney will say something and it reminds me exactly of Lynne when she was that age,' said Britney's aunt Sandra in *Heart to Heart*.

Fate was moving the youngster more in the direction of dancing and singing. Her mother remembers the exact moment she realized her daughter had serious pipes. Britney was out in the garden, bouncing around on the trampoline. She was singing a Sinéad O'Connor song and even tailoring her jumps to the melody – when she had to hit a high note she would jump especially high, the heights of the jumps matching the heights of the notes. This casually but convincingly choreographed performance made Lynne stop and think that she had a serious talent in the family.

Still, it would take a while for her to recognize this fully. Speaking to Oprah Winfrey, Lynne agreed that lots of mothers believe their children have what it takes to become a star. 'Yeah, they do, and that's why it took me a while [to realize it],' she said. 'I knew she was special really like around four. But then by the time she was seven I started really seeing star quality on the stage, because she was a shy child but when she'd get on the stage she had a totally different personality.'

Britney remembered that she'd try to perform when her mother had friends over to their home. 'When she would have friends over, I was always dancing and she was like, "Shut up, Britney, we have company over,"' she told MTV. 'I was always entertaining or performing.' Sometimes the singing sounded so good the visitors assumed a radio was playing. As for Lynne, she remembered that Britney would be very offended 'if you didn't just drop everything to watch her!'

With this sort of understanding, Britney and her mother remained close. In *Heart to Heart* Britney remarks that what she and her mother had between them was 'something rare'. She added, 'Growing up, I knew so many girls who used to fight all the time with their moms – over everything, it seemed: boys, clothes, curfews – and that used to make me sad.' In the same book, Lynne wrote that 'Britney and I would go to the moon for each other'.

When she was four, Britney swapped her bathroom-based fan club of dolls and teddy bears for a new audience: the congregation at a local church. The First Baptist was not the nearest church to the family home, that was Greenlaw Church, but it was at First Baptist that she stood up and sang in public for the first time.

It was a big moment for her. She had sung in the church's junior choir before, but she was very nervous when it was time for her first solo slot, which came at a Christmas service. She sang 'What Child Is This?', a song that celebrates with wonder the birth of Jesus Christ. Melodically, it is set to the tune of 'Greensleeves'.

Britney showed her nerves when she slanted her head to one side as she sang, but that could not diminish the quality of her voice. Lynne wrote that her daughter 'just blew everyone away', with the whole town unable to stop talking about 'how great' she was. Before long the whole world would be saying the same of Britney.

As her singing teacher said of her, she had a 'big belt voice' as a kid. Meanwhile, Britney, a future pop idol, was acquiring heroes of her own. 'I did really admire Whitney Houston,' she told *Variety*. 'I thought she was everything, and Janet Jackson, oh my goodness.' She was also a fan of Madonna and Mariah Carey. Lynne used to have the radio on loud when the two were in the car, and Britney would sing along. Britney's admiration for Madonna would continue and mark her career in several ways, including when the two pop icons famously kissed during an awards ceremony and when the older woman supported Britney in her fight against her conservatorship.

Further public performances came at school events, including Grandparents Day, where Britney would belt out the national anthem. She also sang at a 'fish fry' event in the school diner. Britney competed in her first talent show when she was six. It was at a dairy festival in Kentwood. Wearing a top hat and wielding a cane, she looked adorable and won comfortably.

Lynne recalled that she was proud of her daughter's victory but even prouder of how she conducted herself in such a potentially overwhelming situation. She showed she could also prevail in much tougher contests when she was the winner at the Miss Talent Central States Competition, where she was up against strong opposition in the form of girls from Texas, Alabama, Mississippi and Louisiana.

All the while, Britney was attending a Christian school called Parklane Academy, in the nearby town of McComb, Mississippi, which had the motto 'excellence in Christian education'. The small private school had been formed relatively recently, in the 1970s. It was a single-storey building of corrugated iron with a very religiously influenced curriculum. Even maths questions would feature stories from the Bible. Indeed, every morning at 8 a.m., a teacher would read a passage from the Bible. Preachers would arrive from pro-abstinence groups such as the True Love Waits campaign, and students were also taught the theory of creationism in classrooms featuring crucifixes.

Teachers told Britney and the other pupils to 'thank God for all your many blessings', adding that if you 'give God your best, he will help with the rest'. The school uniform was red and blue with a 'P' logo embossed on it and was more demure than the uniform she would infamously wear in the video for her debut hit '… Baby One More Time'. She wore it as she took a yellow bus to school for the twenty-five-minute journey. Britney had 'tons of friends' and remembers her school days as 'so much fun'. She was not a wild pupil but not a model one either. 'I was never a teacher's pet because I talked way too much in class,' she told Jo Whiley, adding that she was once spanked because she was talking too much. 'I was so devastated,' she added. Having said that, her grades were good – a mixture of As and Bs.

Back home, things were not so shiny for Britney and her family, who were struggling financially. They were frequently unable to pay bills, and energy companies would threaten to cut them off. When their heater broke down, the family was unable to fix or replace it. They shivered through two successive winters with just small gasoline heaters. When they exhaled they could see their breath. Britney would go to the fridge and find it empty.

Jamie would venture out into the woods behind the home and hunt food for the family to eat for their dinner. According to *Britney: Inside the Dream* by Steve Dennis, this sometimes meant she ate rabbit or squirrel for dinner. Sometimes Lynne had to borrow money from friends. The phone company cut them off, a symbolic humiliation for them, capping some very difficult times for the Spears family.

Jamie and Lynne were always open with their children about the problems they were facing. The pipes were leaking, the paint peeling and their homeware crumbling, but, they told the kids, as long as they continued to love each other then they had the most important thing. They also tried to turn the hardship into a learning experience that if the kids wanted something, they would have to work and earn the money for it – a message that would form the lyrics for one of Britney's biggest hits, 'Work Bitch'.

Britney took this suggestion and ran with it during her later career, but in the meantime she learned how to spot a bargain. Lynne remembered proudly how her daughter would shop at sales and discount racks, somehow assembling outfits that made her look a million bucks even though they cost less than $20. Other clothes came her way from friends who offered her hand-me-downs from their own family collections.

She took part in a school production of *Give Thanks America* and in a later performance sang a solo rendition of 'Lavender's Blue'. In the audience for that latter performance was Britney's baby sister, Jamie Lynne, who was born on 4 April 1991 in McComb. Lynne remembered that news of her pregnancy had been a surprise for her and Jamie – 'the shock of our lives'. They thought they were 'done' with having kids and there was 'no way' they would have planned a third pregnancy, she admitted.

Jamie Lynn herself wrote in her memoir *Things I Should Have Said* that she was an 'oops'. With Bryan twelve and Britney nine, their mum and dad had decided not to have any more children. Jamie had even undergone a vasectomy. But then Lynne woke up one morning and didn't feel right. When a doctor examined her, she was told she was pregnant. This came as quite the shock given the procedure Jamie had undergone, but the mystery was solved when it transpired he had not gone for a post-op check-up. Lynne was less than pleased and did not speak to her husband for weeks.

Nevertheless, Britney was thrilled to have a baby sister. This made Britney a middle child, who according to birth-order theories are often excluded, ignored or even outright neglected. Given how the family threw their support around Britney's childhood dreams, there is precious little evidence of 'middle child syndrome' being a factor in the Spears family. And Britney was almost hypnotized by her sister. Lynne Spears wrote in her memoir *Through the Storm* of how Britney would gaze 'in adoration' at her baby sister, 'holding her blanketed bundle with all the care and attention of a mother'.

Jamie Lynn has written that Britney 'became our momma's extra set of hands', who 'did everything – bathing, feeding, playtime, and diaper changing'. Although both Britney and Bryan had their own lives to lead, they 'always made time for her', she wrote. Britney was, by Lynne's own admission, better at 'the girlie things', writes Jamie Lynn. She would make sure her little sister looked 'perfectly adorable'.

'From the day I arrived,' she wrote, 'I became Britney's.' With Lynne busy working, Britney became a second mother to Jamie Lynn. 'She was considerably older than I was, and she adored having the role of caregiver. Momma was wonderful, but my sister treated me like I was her very own American Girl doll.' Noting her younger sister's theatrical tendencies, Britney encouraged and nurtured them. Jamie Lynn credits this with her developing the confidence to perform in front of others.

Taking the reader into the home she and her siblings grew up in, Britney's sister says the family was 'big on togetherness and long on love'. She added that family and friends 'filled our backyard every weekend' and the kids would play under a big tree in the centre of the yard. The barbecue grill would be sizzling and neighbours would pop in and out of the yard. Or sometimes the kids would pop next door to their neighbour's yard, where there was a pool to swim in.

After Jamie Lynn was born, her father went on a health kick, cutting out the drink and working out hard at the gym he ran in the area. Sometimes, Britney would appear and change the atmosphere. Local men who had been weight-lifting to the strains of country music would suddenly hear pop music filling the air and see Britney dancing. Even the men who were sitting in the steam room were not safe; Britney would walk in dressed in a bikini and start practising the operatic notes she was learning at the time.

Britney also sang at the wedding of her Aunty Chanda, who was marrying her uncle John Mark Spears. The ceremony was held at the Nazarene Church in Magnolia, Mississippi. She sang the Naomi Judd song 'Love Can Build a Bridge', and her aunt was impressed. 'Oh Lord, she was better back then than she is today,' Chanda has said. 'She needs to recapture her natural voice because that child could sing, let me tell you. She had a gorgeous voice, one that sent chills through everyone who heard her. She was breathtaking, and don't let people tell you no different.'

It was time for her to take that breathtaking voice and see how wide an audience she could get for it. At eight years of age, Britney auditioned for popular TV show *The All-New Mickey Mouse Club*. A friend had given her the heads-up, passing her a newspaper clipping of an advert for open auditions in Atlanta, Georgia. The producers were looking for average kids with extraordinary talents.

Britney was inspired and excited by the chance to take part. She was determined to be there and convinced Lynne to drive her the 500 miles. In the car, Britney continued her rehearsals for the audition, belting out her chosen song, 'Sweet Georgia Brown', during the eight-hour drive. It was quite a journey, even once the driving was over: they had to wait another eight hours once they arrived before, finally, Britney's moment came. Wearing a black-and-white leotard, she sang her song. She also performed some backflips, to showcase more of her ability and repertoire. Casting director Matt Casella later remarked that Britney had blown him away with her 'comfort' and 'authority'. Writing on MySpace, he said Britney was 'the most talented eight-year-old I ever auditioned', a 'one-of-a-kind kid'.

Of the thousands who auditioned, she was one of just half a dozen to be put through. Although she impressed the panel at the next audition, they decided that she was too young to be put forward. Indeed, those who eventually got put through for the show were all around five years older than Britney. Another singer who had made an impression at the auditions but who proved to be too young to get the nod on the day was one Christina Aguilera.

Nevertheless, Britney continued working hard and preparing in every way she could think of for a career in show-business. She was determined: when she went to the dentist at the age of eight, she told her she had to have a really beautiful smile because she was going to be a star. She was building what her sister later described as an 'impressive résumé' and wanted to take it out to the world.

Although she had been rejected by the *All-New Mickey Mouse Club*, the man who closed that door opened a new one for Britney just months later. In 1990, Casella asked his assistant, Jean, to phone a leading New York agent and tell her about this talented youngster they had seen. For that agent, a recommendation from Casella was a rare thing, so she immediately paid attention.

From her office on Broadway, Nancy Carson had guided the careers of a galaxy of successful stars, including Ben

Affleck, Matt Damon, Cynthia Nixon and Mischa Barton. She knew what she was looking for in young hopefuls. As she wrote in her memoir *Raising a Star*, Carson thought the top three qualities were motivation, a winning look and talent. She found all three in Britney.

After the call from Jean, Carson received another from Lynne Spears. She told the eager mother to send her a letter and a video. Jamie penned the letter, telling Carson that his daughter was keen and willing to work hard. The family enclosed a video of Britney singing a range of songs, including 'Shine On, Harvest Moon', 'Cry', 'Nothing Compares 2 U' and 'This Is My Moment'.

Carson was impressed with all the tracks with the exception of 'This Is My Moment'. She felt Britney was a little off-pitch with that one. However, she was impressed enough overall to phone Jamie and Lynne and tell them she would be happy to meet them if they could travel to New York. This was no simple task for the Spears family. They were unable to fly because Lynne was then pregnant with Jamie Lynn and the expense would be too much. So, they chose to make the 1,300-mile journey by train.

The travelling party was seven strong: as well as Britney and her parents were Bryan, his friend Hunter and Britney's aunt Jeanine and cousin Tara. Britney and her group of supporters squeezed into a two-bed sleeper carriage for the journey, which lasted more than twenty-six hours. As they travelled, the doubting statements of her neighbours echoed in Lynne's head. They had told her she must be 'out of her mind' to be taking her precious daughter to New York, a place considered violent and sinful by many Americans.

It was certainly a world away from where they lived. As they emerged from New York's Pennsylvania Station into Midtown Manhattan, they were all wide-eyed and overwhelmed by the noisy, crowded surroundings. The buildings were so tall, the people were so busy and the roads were jammed and noisy. According to legend, Britney looked around and asked where all the cows were. The Spears party were on a tight budget: they stayed in a single hotel room and walked everywhere to save on fares. It was raining and they had just one umbrella between them. The degree of sacrifice they were willing to go through was huge.

Then it was time for the big meeting. When they arrived at Carson's offices, the agent asked to see Britney on her own first. The youngster made a quick impression. 'She walked through the door, and she was shy,' remembered Carson. However, speaking to the *Pittsburgh-Post Gazette*, she added, 'The moment she was asked to perform, this amazing little performer just started up – she evolved on the spot.' The sacrifice had been worth it: Britney had nailed the audition.

However, one issue stood out: the overarching southern-ness of Britney, in both her voice and her manners. She answered all Carson's questions 'Yes, ma'am' or 'No, ma'am.' It was too much. Amusingly, when Carson pulled her up on this and asked her to rein it in a bit, Britney's response showed there was a mountain to climb. 'Yes, ma'am,' she said. Getting her to vary her patter would obviously be a bit of a project.

When Jamie and Lynne joined them in the room, they asked Carson to give it to them straight: did their daughter have a hope of becoming a star? They could not afford financially or emotionally to keep pursuing this dream if it was hopeless. She told them Britney might have a chance and that she should spend a summer in the Big Apple to her hone her craft and attend some auditions. In short, she had definite potential, but she needed some coaching.

For the Spears family this was a big challenge financially. Carson told them to give it some thought, but she also gave it to them straight, adding that nothing could be guaranteed, so they shouldn't 'sell the farm'. Nevertheless, Lynne arranged for her, Britney and Britney's newly born little sister to decamp to New York to chase Britney's dream. They settled in a cramped apartment off 48th Street in the theatre district. From there, they could reach by foot the various venues where Britney would be polishing her skills. There was the Professional Performing Arts School, the Broadway Dance Center and Carson's agency office. Britney would walk alongside her mum, who would be pushing Jamie Lynn in a stroller. Her mother was a picture of selflessness and support in those days. Carson remembered the regular sight of Lynne struggling out of the lift in her office with a stroller and Britney.

It was on these days that Britney and her mother would put in the hard work that would, eventually, pay off. They moved between different budget apartments, always looking for a better deal. Britney took singing lessons with Gene McLaughlin and another vocal coach called Robert Marks.

She learned more dance moves at the Broadway Dance Center, under the watchful eye of a choreographer called Frank Hatcher. Her work ethic again helped her to impress.

Here, Britney was being invited to take her ambitions to a new level. The implicit question being asked of her in every class was: how much do you really want this? The answer kept coming back that she really, really wanted it. Her coaches remarked on how professional and focused she was. These tutors were no strangers to ambitious young hopefuls, but Britney stood out as someone who wanted to go all the way and who was prepared to put in the hours and sweat required to get there. Carson described the Britney of those days as a little sponge who would soak up everything she needed to learn.

Meanwhile, she was also being tested at auditions. She tried out for a part in *Les Misérables* and then for an off-Broadway production called *Ruthless! The Musical*. In an example of life (somewhat) imitating art, the musical was about a young girl who will stop at nothing to land the lead part in a school production. Britney originally tried out for a smaller part, rather than the lead role. She was not successful, but there was a twist when the young actress who had got the bigger part dropped out. Britney was invited back to serve as understudy for the lead.

Sadly for Britney, Laura Bell Bundy, the actress who was playing the lead, rarely missed a show. So, although Britney had to be in costume and ready to roll, she did not set foot on stage much. However, at one point Bundy was absent for a short while to film a movie role and Britney finally got to step out on stage and take the lead at the 248-seat Players Theater in Greenwich Village. One of her co-stars told broadway.com that Britney had 'a big voice'.

But, for most nights of the run, Britney would simply watch from the wings, all dressed up with nowhere to go. She and Lynne would arrive back at the apartment close to midnight. She said later that the understudy gig got boring for her. Having to know every line by heart and be ready at a second's notice to be on stage became too much. As Christmas approached, these unsatisfying groundhog days combined with missing home. A replacement was found for her part in the production.

Back home in Kentwood, Britney began to pass the usual milestones of adolescence. She met a friend of her brother's called Donald Reginald Jones, known to most as Reg. He thought Britney, who was three years his junior, seemed a bit too young, but within a few years they would be an item. First, though, she had a talent show to compete in.

Chapter Two

MICKEY MOUSE

Two decades before the likes of *American Idol* and the *X Factor* parked their considerable juggernauts in TV schedules, with Britney herself appearing as a judge on the latter franchise, a rather gentler talent contest captivated US television audiences. *Star Search* was launched in 1983 and had ten different categories, from dance to comedy and the more curious 'spokesmodel', aiming to tap into the feeling of the American dream. It initially ran until 1995, with a rebooted version broadcast in 2003 and 2004, cashing in on the success of the modern talent show trend.

At the heart of the show was a head-to-head between two acts, watched over by four judges who would rank each performance with full stars, three-quarter stars, half stars or quarter stars. Compared to modern talent shows, with their cynical and often cruel gimmicks thrown in to keep ratings high, there was a kindly and wholesome atmosphere. Of course, there were disappointments for some hopefuls, but the overall feeling was supportive.

A grand prize of $100,000 was up for grabs for the winner of the adult categories, with $10,000 for junior stars. Among its alumni are big names such as Christina Aguilera, Rosie O'Donnell, Justin Timberlake, Usher … and Britney

Spears. It was a big deal for Britney to take part. Her mother Lynne, who flew with Britney to Los Angeles for the finals, said it was 'probably the first major thing that we thought she had ever done'.

For her first performance, Britney had sung 'I Don't Care'. She looked so small and young for a ten-year-old, but her performance was sassy, complete with knowing smiles and a self-assured wagging of her finger, and the vocals were spot on. It had been a confident showing. She won an overall mark of 3.75 and marched into the next round. Asked how she felt to progress, she said simply, 'I feel wonderful.' Even before she had media training, Britney knew to keep it simple in her first television interview.

Although the next round was portrayed on-screen as taking place a week later, it was actually filmed hours after Britney's first victory. Here, things would not go so smoothly for the young star.

The country song she sang, 'Love Can Build a Bridge', is one for mature vocalists who have been through the mill romantically. It is asking a lot of any child to be able to embody the weariness of the tune. Vocally, Britney does as well as any ten-year-old could be expected to, but the unsuitability of the song casts a shadow of discomfort.

Towards the end of the tune, she shrugged this off and delivered some powerful vocals, but the song choice had proven to be a handicap. Her team had tried to convince the show's producers to change it, but Britney was stuck with it, and this allowed her challenger, Marty Thomas, to shine. He won by the narrowest margin possible: a quarter star.

As the result was announced, Britney tried her best to smile, but her exhalation showed her bitter disappointment. She hugged Thomas before she had to leave the stage. Backstage, she burst into tears and curled up on a sofa as she continued to cry.

Britney wasn't just crying in a melodramatic way – she was genuinely heartbroken. Over and over in her head, she asked herself what she had done wrong. She also thought about people back home in Kentwood. They would have tuned in to watch, and she felt mortified about facing them. Although Lynne's heart ached for Britney, she told her daughter to show Thomas that she was pleased for him and to be a good sport.

It had been a heartbreaking end to the show. And her experience during the contest threw up another awkward moment that presaged the objectification Britney has experienced throughout her career. The show's host, Ed McMahon, interviewed Spears as the judges decided on their marks. The sixty-nine-year-old told the ten-year-old hopeful she had 'adorable, pretty eyes' and asked her if she had a boyfriend. 'No, sir,' she replied, and he asked her why not. 'Because they're mean,' she said.

McMahon then told her he was not mean and asked if he could be her boyfriend. Visibly and understandably uncomfortable, she replies, 'Well, it depends.' Although there is no suggestion of any impropriety by the late McMahon, it had been an unpleasant exchange and one that has aged badly. However, it would be far from the last time that Britney felt embarrassed over media questions of this sort.

No sooner had Britney stepped back from the spotlight of *Star Search* than she was asked to step right back into it. In 1993, Matt Casella was on the hunt for a fresh cast for the Mickey Mouse Club. There was no shortage of quantity – more than 20,000 children auditioned – but Casella was after quality, so he put in some calls with agents and scouts to see if they could recommend anyone. When he phoned Carson, she reminded him about Britney and told him she had grown up a lot since he last saw her. So, Britney, at the tender age of eleven, was on her way back to New York, where she sang 'Running Back to You'. She was also asked to prepare a speech and opted for a spot of oratory about the tooth fairy.

She was put through to the next round of auditions, which would be held in Orlando, Florida. As she waited, she was thrown a dilemma when the producers of a film called *Gordy* invited her to join the cast. This was tempting for Britney – the chance to appear in a movie! However, she could not do both, and she eventually decided that the Disney path would play more to her strengths, choosing to wait on the Mickey Mouse news.

So, to Orlando, where she was one of twenty-three children trying out for seven places. Among her rivals were three other future stars: Christina Aguilera, Jessica Simpson – and Justin Timberlake. The hopefuls would be marked out of ten in each of six categories: vocals, acting, camera persona, dance, personality and appearance. Britney's marks, of eight for appearance and 8.5 for the others, combined to give her the highest overall score. It had been quite a search, but the producers had found the Mouseketeers they were looking for: fresh-faced hopefuls who 'weren't really agent and Hollywood savvy', as producer Sarah Elgart described them to E! News.

Britney was back in Kentwood when the call came through to tell her she had made the cut. She was excited, and so was the local community. Accordingly, 24 April 1993 was made 'Britney Spears Day'. Local newspapers devoted several pages to Britney and news of her Mickey Mouse gig. Shops put 'congratulations' and 'good luck' messages in their windows, the local baseball club presented her with a cake and a celebratory event was held in a park, where Britney sang 'I Will Always Love You'.

The local mayor released a statement of congratulations, which noted that the town's community had watched Britney 'grow and her talents mature' and remarked that her performances 'give such warmth and noticeable enjoyment'. He invited locals to 'applaud her accomplishments and wish her great things as she takes this next step in her promising career'.

Britney's family responded with a statement of their own. They said that she had enjoyed 'many memorable moments' in her 'short, little life', but this was 'the most sentimental moment yet'. They added, 'Thank you, Kentwood, for your support and encouragement. We love you.' The irony of this huge fuss was that virtually nobody in the town had cable television at the time, and so no one could watch the series they were so excited to see Britney star in.

Britney's weekly pay was going to prove very helpful

to the whole family. Every Thursday, Lynne would be handed a crisp cheque for $1,500 on behalf of her daughter. Opportunities for Jamie had collapsed, and the family was becoming increasingly desperate for money, so the windfalls would have been a welcome relief.

Then it was time for the next chapter. The same trio that went to New York – Britney, Lynne and young Jamie Lynn – set off to Orlando. They settled in an apartment on the outskirts of the city.

On her first day, Britney was brought down to earth when the first task was to meet head tutor Chuck Yerger. He regarded Britney as a friendly, cute, innocent-looking girl. However, he admitted later that he wondered how she had survived the audition process and feared that show business would consume her.

She and her fellow cast members were told that they would be doing three hours' schooling every weekday, following a curriculum from their original schools. Britney would study English, history, social studies and mathematics in the school bungalow, and the close, personal attention of the tutors helped guide her to straight As across the board. On the performance side, they were told they would have to quickly learn and rehearse a show, which would then be performed in front of the older cast members and the crew.

Years later, the media would speculate that Britney and Christina Aguilera were sworn, bitter enemies. However, back in Orlando the two girls were on great terms. There was a sense of competitiveness that benefited both girls. Britney, the better dancer, encouraged Aguilera to move better.

Aguilera, the superior singer, drove Britney to improve her own vocals. Helping them both with their voices was a vocal coach called Robin Wiley, who would put them through their paces in a small room in a mini-trailer.

Britney also looked up to Keri Russell, another cast member. Russell was older than Britney and the younger girl was thrilled to be taken under her wing. The girls would go to the local mall, where Britney would ask Russell for advice about everything from show business to romance. Another cast member, Nikki DeLoach, later told *E! True Hollywood Story* that the young hopefuls had made a secret pact. 'Christina told me that a couple of the younger kids had made a vow to become stars one day and promised each other that they were going to do this.'

As well as looking up to female cast members, Britney was noticing the boys too. She developed a crush on an older cast member, Tony Lucca, who was Russell's boyfriend. He was seventeen at the time and told E! that Britney made quite the impression. The older kids 'would always ask Britney how the [dance] combinations went, because she was really great at committing them to memory', he said. However, she never got anywhere near a relationship with him. 'I don't think it was so much that she had a crush on me as much as it is that she just admired everything about Keri – including Keri's boyfriend,' he said.

She was closer to a boy called Justin Timberlake, grabbing a quick peck with him during a game of truth or dare. She certainly made an impression on the boy: on one visit home he told his grandfather about Britney, adding that one day he would marry her. Born on 31 January 1981 in Memphis, Tennessee, Timberlake had music in the family.

His father was a Baptist church choir director and, among other musicians in the family, his grandfather introduced him to music from country artists like Johnny Cash and Willie Nelson. Before he met Britney at the Mickey Mouse Club, he sang country and gospel music: at the age of eleven, he also appeared on the television show *Star Search*, performing country songs as Justin Randall. That cheeky kiss during truth or dare would be the first sign of a relationship.

The daily experience was not as glamorous as outsiders might assume. She would be woken by 7 a.m. for a twelve-hour day of rehearsals and three hours of non-stop filming. Among the curious coaching they received was how to smile. They would be told to toss their head and drop their lower lip to reveal as many of their whitened teeth as possible. Then there was media training, for which public relations experts from Hollywood would jet in to teach the cast how to give bland answers to interviewers.

Several critics have complained over the years of how anodyne Britney's answers can be during interviews, but from the point of view of those handling her this was a positive attribute. Over the course of six months, she filmed fifty-five shows, but she was back home in Kentwood before any of them were aired. It went out Monday to Thursday at 5.30 p.m. on the Disney Channel. Viewers took to Britney quickly and sent in fan mail praising her dance skills.

One show saw Britney and Timberlake singing Prince's 'I Feel For You' with Dale Godboldo. Britney handled all the powerful notes with aplomb, her short stature belying the big notes she was belting out. Another saw Britney return home to show viewers where she lived. She drove around in go-karts – telling viewers 'I feel the need for speed' – played basketball as she described herself as 'Air Britney' and worked in her grandmother's seafood restaurant ('These are gonna be the best shrimp you ever had'). She even demonstrated how to peel a crawfish. 'The head is the best part,' she said. 'I eat like a horse.'

When she arrived for her second season, she was not aware it would be the final. The show's senior producer gave the news to the youngsters, and there were plenty of tears. There were budgetary issues, and the Disney executives felt that the show had peaked. As for Carson, she told a local Pittsburgh paper that she still loves Britney. Her association has been of great use to the agent. 'I still get a lot of people who want to be clients because of Britney,' she said.

Crew members almost universally describe the Britney of those days as wholesome and innocent, but it seems there was some naughtiness. Lynne Spears believed Britney was drinking not long after she joined the show, reported the *National Enquirer*. Back home, Britney was not above getting in trouble, and sometimes this was because her brother had dobbed her in.

When she was thirteen, Britney was already learning to drive. A rusty old truck the family called the Green Lizard was her chariot for these lessons, which she took alongside her cousin Laura Lynne and always with an adult present. Well, almost always.

One night, the two girls snuck out of the house and drove the Green Lizard around the block. Bryan reported this to their parents and Britney was in big trouble. She was grounded and ordered to clean the yard. 'I can still see her, stomping around the yard, picking up sticks and things, and shoving them in a bucket, with tears streaming down her face,' wrote Lynne. 'She was so mad at Bryan!'

Bryan also grassed on Britney when she and some of her friends snuck over to a boy's house in McComb. He and a friend followed the girls and reported what was going on. She was grounded and ordered to walk around the neighbourhood with a bucket, picking up litter. Bryan took photographs of her as she tearfully fulfilled the punishment. He didn't want her to forget how much trouble you get into when you are naughty, especially as she was growing up so fast.

When she was fourteen, Britney started dating Reg Jones, Bryan's friend she had met a few years previously. He had the homecoming ceremony coming up, and despite his good looks and impressive, sporty physique, he was lacking a date. One day, he asked Britney if she thought her dad would mind him taking her to the dance; Britney said she would ask him. Jamie summoned Reg to help him clean crawfish at Granny's seafood deli, and following an awkward conversation, permission was granted. However, Reg recalled, although Jamie was okay with it, Bryan was not as at ease with the prospect of Reg dating his little sister.

On the night of the homecoming, Britney wore a pretty black evening gown and they danced during the disco. Reg had been set a 1 a.m. curfew to return her home by, and he made it with ten minutes to spare. As his relationship with Britney continued, he had other rules to abide by. As his girlfriend was under the age of fifteen, she was legally of 'chaperone age'. This meant that they needed to have an adult present when they were together. When there was no adult to watch over them, they would be asked to look after young Jamie Lynn, on the basis that there was less likely to be mischief if they were on babysitting duties.

Their first kiss came after Reg had sent Britney a bunch of roses to commiserate with her because she had failed her driving test. 'It's okay, baby, you'll get it next time,' he wrote on the accompanying card. At a party later that day, Britney thanked him for the roses, and they shared a kiss, with Britney having to stand on tiptoes for her lips to reach his. That was a cute moment, but a subsequent snog went less well; it was interrupted by Reg's mother, who told them: 'This doesn't look good and I don't like it.'

On other occasions they went on marathon shopping sessions, which Britney enjoyed somewhat more than Reg. The enjoyment ratios were reversed when Reg took Britney turkey hunting. She was getting attacked by mosquitoes, and her twitching and swatting meant she distracted the birds just as Reg and his friends had them in their sights. Another time he took Britney (and Jamie Lynn) deer hunting. According to an account given by Reg in *Britney: The Unauthorized Biography* by Sean Smith, the couple killed two deer that day. In a particularly ghoulish detail, Jamie Lynn is said to have tried to pet one of the carcasses, not fully realizing it was dead.

When Britney was fifteen, Reg got a taste of her caring side when he fell ill during a trip the couple took with his mother. They had ventured to Colorado, and at first all went well. The teenage couple went rollerblading and water rafting, but then Reg got food poisoning and spent the rest of the vacation sick in bed. For days, Britney refused to leave his side, apart from one brief excursion to buy him some fresh clothes. She held the sick bucket in position as Reg vomited over and over. True devotion.

He, in turn, could be gallant. He paid for everything when they went out and bought her jewellery including a ring and a necklace. She cheered him on from the stands when he played football; he held her hand when she wept her way through the soppy movies they went to see together. At night they would sit by the lake and look up at the stars. It all seemed so perfect and romantic – but suspicion and jealousy were just around the corner, ready to get their claws into this young love.

The grapevine sent messages to Reg that Britney was playing around and messages to Britney that Reg had been unfaithful. Another complication came when Lynne began to grow resentful of Britney's relationship with Reg. She worried that Britney would be distracted from her path in life by settling down too young.

Meanwhile, her nascent career rolled on. As wannabe stars try to rise to the top, there are often cases of near-misses. Diversions that almost happened. For some hopefuls, these are cases of them missing out on that golden opportunity; for others, they are dodged bullets, chances it was good luck that they missed. When Britney came within an inch of joining a band hoping to become America's answer to Girls Aloud, it was definitely a case of a bullet dodged.

It was Justin Timberlake's mother, Lynn Harless, who had the vision of launching a fresh girl band. In 1997, she had noted the success her son was already enjoying in boy band *NSYNC and wanted to put together a female equivalent. A band she would name Innosense. Nikki DeLoach, who Britney knew from the Mickey Mouse days, was the first member to be snapped up by Harless. Britney, who was nearly sixteen, was supposed to be the next one. Lynn phoned Lynne, and before anyone knew it Britney was flying up to the Timberlake home in Memphis to discuss plans and shake on an agreement. There was significant money behind the idea because Lou Pearlman, the millionaire behind the Backstreet Boys, was bankrolling it. Britney posed for photos with her putative bandmates.

Just twenty-four hours before Britney was due to sign her contract, Harless got a call telling her that Jamie didn't want his daughter to join a band, as he saw her future as a solo artist. Innosense did not prove to be a success, but Britney obviously did okay as a solo singer. Indeed, the band's highest achievement would be performing as an opening support act on Britney's first tour.

By now, Britney was being advised by a new mastermind. Larry Rudolph was a respected entertainment lawyer and a New Yorker through and through: he was born in The Bronx. After graduating from Hofstra University Law School in 1988, he earned his money as an entertainment lawyer and worked his way towards becoming a talent manager.

A plain speaker, he found his new client to be the exact opposite when he first met her. As he later told the *Hollywood Reporter*, Britney was 'introverted' and didn't meet his eye. Pretty much all she said, he remembered, was 'yes, sir' and 'no, sir'. That southern patter was still dominant in her interactions, particularly with strangers who made her feel nervous at first. However, Rudolph had been around the pop block enough times to spot raw talent.

They met at an auspicious time. Britney did not lack support from her family. They had moved her to home-schooling so she could live with the flexibility required for any meetings or auditions that might arise. Jamie was still struggling to find work but made it clear that he was willing to work longer hours and arrange loans from friends if that helped his daughter's dream come true.

But all the love in the world was not going to be enough. What Britney needed was an industry titan with the contacts and clout to take her places. In the form of Rudolph, she felt she had found him. When she was fourteen, she was 'bored', she wrote. 'I wanted to sing again so, with my lawyer in New York, I called him up and said: "Is there anything I can do?"'

There was. Things were about to speed up for the girl in a hurry.

Chapter Three

OH BABY, BABY

On hearing that Britney had itchy feet, Rudolph asked her to send him a demo tape. Britney recalls that she recorded the tape by simply singing into a recording machine held by Lynne. However, her mother has a differing memory, writing in *Through the Storm* that they posted Rudolph a recording of her daughter singing at a wedding. Either way, they also enclosed photographs of Britney, who still looked extra special after the grooming she'd received for the Innosense photoshoot. 'She was the most beautiful girl any record label could hope for,' Rudolph recalled in *Heart to Heart*.

Whatever the origin of the demo tape, it was clear to Rudolph that he needed a more professional recording. He sent her two versions of a Toni Braxton song – one with vocals for Britney to learn, the other stripped of vocals for her to record herself over in a local recording studio. She posted the new tape to Rudolph and crossed her fingers. Rudolph sent the tape to several record labels and publishers. Three were interested: Mercury, Epic and Jive. Rudolph told Britney she would have to perform at the offices of each of the three labels to a room full of record label bosses. They chose three songs for her: 'I Have Nothing', 'Jesus Loves

Me' and 'Amazing Grace'. She would perform one of them to a backing tape and the other two a cappella. At the end of her performance, she bowed.

The auditions were quite an experience. She told the *Hollywood Reporter* it was odd having just a handful of people watching impassively, rather than a cheering crowd of well-wishers. 'It was sort of nerve-wracking because I'm used to singing in front of big crowds and I went in there and there were these ten executive people sitting there and staring at me,' she remembered later. 'I was like, "Oh my goodness, I'm just going to close my eyes and do the best I can."'

Mercury Records were not impressed. Her audition at Epic was also far from ideal from their bosses' point of view. 'She came in, warbled "I Will Always Love You", and I couldn't wait for it to end,' Michael Caplan, Epic Records vice-president of A&R, told author John Seabrook in his book *The Song Machine*. 'Her complexion wasn't great, her voice wasn't great ... so we passed,' he added. A future superstar had slipped through their fingers.

One of the first to respond was Jeff Fenster, a vice-president at Jive Records. It was an independent label founded by Clive Calder in 1981 as a subsidiary to the Zomba Group. It had offices in New York City and Chicago and made a name for itself in the 1980s and 1990s for its successes with hip-hop, R&B and dance acts. Although he noticed that the demo song was not in the correct key for Britney, Fenster heard enough in the recording to want to learn more about this teenager. He called in photographs of Britney and convinced the team to snap her up.

Barry Weiss, president of Jive Records, told *EW* that Fenster came into an A&R meeting brandishing 'a picture of this really pretty young woman on a red and white picnic blanket, almost like a tablecloth from one of those small, local Italian restaurants'. It was not a classic casting pic for a pop label: Weiss said Britney resembled 'Dorothy from Kansas'.

When it came to the audition, Weiss told *EW* that she appeared 'wearing a black cocktail dress and high heels'. 'She really was a good singer,' he said. 'She looked amazing. She was like, fifteen years old. And we kind of thought, Wow, this is really left of center. There's no female pop artist out there right now.'

Steve Lunt, an A&R executive for Jive, told Seabrook: 'Britney was trying to sing like Toni Braxton, which was way too low for her. It sounded pretty awful in places.' He added: 'But when her voice went up high, you could hear the girlish quality, and there was something really appealing about that.' Those childhood days piping out the high notes on the trampoline had come good.

Lunt also saw a congregation of two very different worlds in Britney. 'Her eyes were rolling back in her head as she was singing and I remember thinking to myself, "That is really weird but it's going to look great on video,"' he said. 'It was old-school church meets modern-day sex,' he said. He had just spotted the curious, captivating dichotomy that would dominate Britney's image during the early years of her career: the contradiction between her religious, innocent youth and an underlying hint at wild eroticism.

The truth was that at this stage Britney was rolling her eyes not because she was trying to exude sexiness but simply because she was so nervous, but she gave the best performance she could. At the end, she remembered later, she was greeted with 'complete silence'. That silence would continue for a fortnight after she went home. Then, finally, the phone rang and it was Rudolph at the other end. It was good news.

Rudolph told her that he had agreed a development deal with Jive Records. Fenster had noted that although Spears had no original material and was only fifteen, she had big prospects. 'Her vocal ability and commercial appeal caught me right away, so I signed her,' he said. However, the deal on the table had a ninety-day 'get out' clause, so they could get her off their hands quickly if things did not look likely to work out. Money was always a ruling factor: Calder, the head of Jive, was attracted to Spears partly because he thought he could get her on the cheap, claimed Seabrook.

'This was a very significant moment in pop history: the signing of Britney Spears as a sort of girl-next-door teenager, rather than a Whitney Houston-esque diva,' Seabrook told *EW*. 'One of the calculations there was, Clive Calder was notoriously cheap, and Whitney Houston was notoriously expensive. So Britney Spears seemed like she would be cheap too, because she was just a teenager from Louisiana, and wasn't demanding in any way.'

The next step was to pair her with a winning songwriter, and few have been as victorious as Max Martin. At the time of writing, the Swede has written or co-written twenty-five US number-one songs, including Katy Perry's 'I Kissed a Girl', Maroon 5's 'One More Night' and Taylor Swift's 'Shake It Off' and 'Blank Space'. He is the songwriter with the third-most number-one singles on the chart, behind only John Lennon (twenty-six) and Paul McCartney (thirty-two). He also produced many of the songs he wrote. He has won the American Society of Composers, Authors and Publishers Songwriter of the Year award a record eleven times.

Martin's first big break was with the Backstreet Boys in 1995, and his second was with Britney. The two struck up a rapport and trust quickly. Looking back in 2011, she told *Rolling Stone* of Martin that he 'gets exactly what I am saying when I tell him what I want and don't want musically. His melodies are incredible and he is always coming up with weird sounds, which I love.'

Speaking to *EW*, he remembered the first time he met Britney. 'I was in Florida and Jeff [Fenster] asked me to stop by the office in New York to meet this girl while I was in America,' he said. He remembered that she was 'all dressed up' and sixteen, whereas the twenty-something Martin seemed to her a 'fifty-year-old producer from the old school'. Recalling that same meeting during an interview with the *Guardian*, Britney said, 'I was pretty young at the time, so I was nervous but he was so nice and put me right at ease.'

She was sent to Martin's Cheiron studios in Stockholm to start recording. The journey meant leaving behind her normal life and all who lived in it. On the eve of her departure, she penned Reg a letter, and soon after she arrived she sent him a postcard. The difference, in length and tone, between the two notes is revealing of the journey she was on and how it would affect the normal parts of her life. 'Well, I'm getting ready to go to Sweden and I'm really excited,' she wrote before she left. 'I just wish you could come with me. That would be great.'

It was a beautiful, developed and seemingly heartfelt note. However, once she was settled in Sweden, she sent Reg a postcard with the curt message: 'I'm missing you lots, but too busy to talk to you as much as I want to.' The two had attempted to keep in touch by phone, but Reg's mother put her foot down when they received a phone bill for $1,500.

Long-distance relationships often flounder not just because of the space in miles but the gap in lived experience. This was the beginning of the end for the couple. There is some confusion over exactly when they went from being an item to becoming separated, but in due course they would split when Reg's suspicions over Britney seeing other guys boiled over.

With her becoming ever more recognized and climbing higher and higher up the showbiz ladder, his jealousies got the better of him. According to *Britney: The Unauthorized Biography* by Sean Smith, Reg shouted at her: 'You're nothing but a f**king bitch' – and with that uncompromising verdict, their relationship was over. There was no coming back from that. Britney had grown tired of his insecurities, but she was nevertheless sad that things had not worked out. At one point after the break-up, she said she doubted she would ever again love somebody as much as she had loved Reg.

While she was away, she was also speaking to her mother by phone. In her memoir *Through the Storm*, Lynne writes that she and her daughter had 'both cried our eyes out' when Britney left for Sweden. They then had 'tearful long-distance phone calls, each of us taking turns telling the other how much she was missed'. Sometimes, wrote Lynne, they would speak up to eight times a day, which left little time for Britney to stand at the mic (and, indeed, little time to send more than a perfunctory postcard to Reg).

For Britney was busy. She would typically arrive in the recording studio at 2 p.m. and not leave until twelve hours later, with only one break, for food, at 7 p.m. She turned sixteen while she was in Sweden, and Martin's co-producer Rami Yacoub remembered how the sweet veneer dropped to reveal a ruthless and hard-working interior. He has said that although she was 'very shy and super sweet', the team 'had no idea there was a beast of an artist lurking under that innocent look'. An early sign of her work ethic came when, after she had been in the recording booth for eight hours, Martin heard her stomach growl in the microphone. He asked if she was hungry. 'No, I'm fine,' she replied. Nevertheless, he insisted upon a break, during which Britney hungrily devoured three burgers.

She was working on a song that would launch her with a bang. Martin said he originally wrote the track on his dictaphone. He was falling asleep when the melody came into his head. 'I remember listening back to [the tape] after [the song] blew up and you can hear me sort of go: "Hit me baby one more time," then I hear myself say, "Yeah, it's pretty good,"' he told Swedish journalist Jan Gradvall. 'I came up with the melody first,' he said. It was Yacoub who gave the song its edge. 'He is much more urban and R&B than me,' he said. 'I'm more of a melody man. So he's a big reason that the song turned out the way that it did.'

The song had already enjoyed quite a journey. Martin originally wrote it for TLC, an American girl group, but they had rejected it. (As band member T-Boz said in 2013: 'Was I going to say, "Hit me baby one more time"? Hell no!') So too had the Backstreet Boys when it was offered to them. Then the Arista label wanted Canadian singer Deborah Cox to record it; however, Martin was not keen on the idea. In a last-minute bid, Simon Cowell asked for a rewritten version of the song for his new boyband, Five. Cowell was so keen on the track he offered Martin a new Merc 500 SL in return for the song. But Martin refused and said he was saving it for a girl called Britney Spears. 'You're mad,' Cowell said of the plan to give it to Britney, according to one of his biographers, Tom Bower. 'No one can be successful with a name like that.' Not one of the talent show judge's finer verdicts.

The song belonged to Britney, and she was delighted. 'I knew it was a great song,' Britney told the *Guardian* later. 'It was different and I loved it, [but] I don't think you can anticipate how a song is going to be received.' Britney's vocal style on the song is curious and a key factor in its sticky appeal. John Seabrook said the approach came about because she was trying to replicate Martin's style in the demo tape. 'Max has an amazing voice, and very few people have ever actually heard that demo,' he told *EW*. 'I did hear it, and Max sounds exactly like Britney, including all the little sounds that sound improvised; the mow-woww sounds. So Britney ended up sounding exactly like Max.'

Another influence on her vocals came from a British pop act from the 1980s. Speaking to *Rolling Stone* in 2000, Britney said she spent the night before the main recording session listening to Soft Cell's 'Tainted Love'. The 1981 cover had transformed the song into a gay anthem, and she thought it a 'sexy song', aiming for just that sort of feel for her own single.

'I wanted my voice to be kind of rusty,' she said. 'I wanted my voice to just be able to groove with the track. So the night before, I stayed up really, really late, so when I went into the studio, I wasn't rested. When I sang it, I was just laid back and mellow – it sounds cool, though. You know, how it sounds really low in the lower register – it sounds really sexy. So I kept telling myself, "Britney, don't get any rest."'

Weiss admitted that, at first, he was unconvinced by the 'Oh bay-bay bay-bay' ad libs that Britney had delivered. 'We thought it was really weird at first,' he told *EW*. 'It was strange. It was not the way Max wrote it. But it worked! We thought it could be a really good opening salvo for her.' It was a good decision: to this day, when people think of Britney Spears, they often think of those memorable 'oh bay-bay bay-bay' vocals.

The song was becoming more iconic the longer they worked on it, and everyone was expected to keep up. Nana Hedin, a backing vocalist, remembered that she tried to fit in with Britney's idiosyncratic vocal style. 'I tried to sound exactly like her,' she told the *Guardian*. 'It was hard, but a lot of fun. I'm like a parrot in many ways. I try to get the same vibe and use the exact same pronunciation as the artist.'

It took between two and three weeks to complete the song, and the work paid off when the final product was cut. Britney and the team were absolutely thrilled with how the track turned out. The only concern they had was over the song's hook of 'hit me baby one more time'. It was feared that it might be seen as an allusion to, or even endorsement of, domestic violence. For Martin, the 'hit me' was meant to refer to a phone call or message, as in 'hit me up'. He refused to change the lyrics, but a compromise of sorts was reached when the track's title had the 'hit me' removed, so it read: '… Baby One More Time'.

By September 1998, the song was ready to hit the airwaves, where it would instantly grab the attention of listeners and go on to make history. In the space of just three minutes and thirty-one seconds, said the *Guardian*, Spears 'launched millennial teen pop, fusing family-friendly, girl-next-door fun with good old fashioned controversy, forging a template for those who followed'. Britney's debut has stayed with her, but it has since also enjoyed quite a journey of its own. It has been covered by bands as varied as Travis, the Dresden Dolls and Tori Amos. On television, it has featured on music drama *Glee* and reality TV show *Popstars*, where contestant Darius Danesh delivered an extraordinary over-the-top cover. That version became so legendary that Britney herself later re-enacted it on British television.

Before all that, the next stage was to crank up the promotional energy for the song and send Britney on a tour of twenty-six cities. She would visit shopping malls to perform and drum up interest, in a series of shows sponsored by teen magazines. Such tours had helped introduce other acts to the public, including Tiffany, when she launched her debut song 'I Think We're Alone Now'. Compared to the extravagant stage productions she would enjoy on some of her later tours, these were appropriately humble shows. Britney, in a preview of the video that would be shot for the single, wore a school tie and had just two backing dancers for company on stage.

Meanwhile, the radio pluggers from Jive were sending her single to stations nationwide, ahead of its release. The radio station teams loved it. The catchy opening hook and Britney's idiosyncratic vocals were soon echoing around malls as Americans shopped and from their radios as they drove home.

The scale and dedication of the radio effort was a sign that the label had very high hopes for Britney. Rather than just tossing promo copies in the post and hoping for the best, the label got behind the campaign, as radio staff remembered later. 'The label guy brought in a video featuring Britney rehearsing dance moves to the song,' Clarke Ingram, then operations manager and programme director of New York's top forty radio station WPXY, told the *Guardian*. 'This had the desired effect of showing me that Britney had star quality, in addition to having a potential hit record. We went to lunch afterwards, and I committed to adding the song at that time.'

Initially, Britney had reasonably modest ambitions for the song's radio presence. 'I was praying every night,' she said later. '"God, please, help them play it on just my radio station at home." And then they did. Then all of a sudden, it's playing on all the big radio stations in New York. And everything just started happening for me, and I was just like, wow, you know?'

She also travelled to Nashville to perform for bosses from Jive and BMG. All the efforts of Britney and her team were paying off.

She can remember when she first heard her single on the radio. She had just flown in from New York to New Orleans. Lynne was there to pick her up at the airport, and when they got into the car the song started blaring out of the radio. Earlier, Lynne had requested the radio play it. Lynne herself had first heard the song on the radio while working out at the local gym. These were proud moments for mother and daughter.

For the video, the label called in a director called Nigel Dick, who had directed for the Backstreet Boys, *NSYNC, Tears for Fears and Oasis. He flew to New York to meet Britney, but his initial idea for the video did not land well with her, as he admitted on his own website. 'I wrote an idea which sucked, so the label put me back on the phone with Britney, who told me she wanted to make a video where she was stuck in a classroom thinking about boys and we took it from there,' he wrote.

That initial idea was for Britney to be a superhero mix of Warrior Princess and Power Ranger, but Britney told the director she thought a video of her in a classroom daydreaming about boys would work better. Britney would prove to be an artist who, by mainstream pop standards at least, was not afraid to speak up for what she wanted.

The video would be filmed at Venice High School, where the movie *Grease* was shot. Britney would be walking and dancing in the footsteps of Olivia Newton-John and John Travolta. The video saw Britney transform from a coy, small-town southern girl into an electrified, sexually confident performer. She tied her white school blouse into a knot so her navel was on display and danced suggestively, pouting at the camera. Sure, teenage girls would relate to her and teenage boys would fancy her, but there seemed to be little concern about how older viewers would respond to this provocative schoolgirl. Along with the song's 'hit me' lyric, this was a problematic element to the world's first sighting of Britney.

Despite her initially modest expectations, the song sold 500,000 copies on its first day of release in the US and ultimately peaked at number one. It reached the top of the hit parade in every single country it charted in and was 1999's biggest selling song in the UK, with over 1.4 million copies sold. When it debuted at number one in the US charts, the family was 'absolutely shell-shocked, no one more than me', wrote Lynne.

So, the single was already in the hands – and ears – of teenage girls when Britney joined *NSYNC as the opening act of their tour. This is a tough slot to take at a boy band's concert, because the fans are there to see their heroes and don't want anyone – least of all a girl – getting in the way of that. Britney remembered when she had been in the audience of a Backstreet Boys concert and seen first-hand the fans drowning out the support act with chants.

Taking to the stage at the *NSYNC tour's opening show in Florida, she heard a few boos from the audience. 'There were all these girls in the audience,' Britney remembered in a chat with *Billboard*, 'but I was able to win them over in the end. I have guy dancers and believe me, that helps!' Her catchy debut single went a long way to help too. Those who had heard it already could join in, and others took to it quickly. She could see fans singing along and thought this was 'really cool'.

Indeed, a keen student of these shows as they played out, Britney quickly recognized that the pressure was strongest on the headliners. 'I had the advantage that I wasn't the main act and I was able to do my little show and get back on the bus. I didn't have all that pressure on me like they did,' she said. For a budding star so young, this showed an awareness that would stand her in good stead.

The *Milwaukee Journal Sentinel* mentioned Britney in their review of the show. 'Spears' amiable voice and solid stage presence were more than enough to carry inane material about crushes, and her twenty-minute set was full of hints that a more interesting vocalist may one day break through her sugar shell,' wrote Gemma Tarlach in a reasonably prescient verdict.

It was during this tour that Britney first started getting serious with Justin Timberlake. Having kissed her co-star during a game of truth or dare back in the Mickey Mouse Club days, Britney got serious with him as they travelled around the country. The relationship was kept secret because both of them – but particularly Timberlake – had to maintain a pretence of being single and therefore available to fans. In Britney's case, the higher priority was to avoid alienating herself from Timberlake's admirers by being linked to him.

Britney would tell anyone who asked that she simply didn't have enough time to have a boyfriend. Meanwhile, Timberlake would reply to such questions with a joke. 'I am actually dating Britney,' he would say. 'We've been together for seven years. I'm dating her and two of her dancers.' Given that accusations of infidelity were eventually to break the couple up, this early quip has not aged well.

They would meet up at exclusive hotels in Los Angeles or in a club called Dublin's, which was just off Sunset Boulevard. Onlookers have recalled that Britney was very low key and shy on these occasions. Others portray her as hopelessly naïve, forever lost in awe at the reasonably unremarkable fact that Timberlake, a musical performer, played both the piano and the guitar.

Jamie Lynn has recalled her own take on the relationship in her memoir – and it's a happy take. 'Plain and simple, I adored Justin,' she wrote, because he was 'my first example of a kind and generous young man'. She added that Timberlake was 'always so sweet to me, and his relationship with Britney was the only one in my life that gave me a sense of stability'. Jamie Lynn said he treated her like a little sister and 'doted on [her] any chance he got'.

She wrote that Timberlake knew that she liked to create 'skits' and thought the camera would be a useful creative outlet for her. 'I appreciated Britney's willingness to make me the third wheel in her relationship and I am eternally grateful for the memories they gave me.'

Some of the happiest moments in this period came when Jamie Lynn lived in a house off Sunset Boulevard, where Britney and Justin had their own place. Jamie Lynn remembered how they would 'hang out as sisters'. They would spend long days in the pool, making up dances and acting out improvised performances and scenes. Once, Britney choreographed an entire routine to the P!nk song 'Get the Party Started'. Britney then directed a video recording of the entire performance. Her little sister remembered 'singing to the camera, being my sassy self' and 'feeling like a star'. It was, she wrote, 'typical of my sister to make me feel cool'.

However, while these times had a free and easy air, Britney eventually became suspicious of Timberlake. She wondered if he was seeing other girls from the industry, including a member of the British girl band All Saints. Others were also wondering if all was well. Lynne began to become sceptical, for instance. She was unimpressed when her daughter began to show signs of questioning her Christian faith following conversations with Justin. On one occasion, Britney said to her mother: 'Mama, I just don't know if there really is a right and a wrong anymore. I mean, is anything really wrong?' When the young lovers began to discuss buying a house together when they were just nineteen and unmarried, Lynne was also upset.

So, we can only imagine Lynne's reaction when, during media speculation that her daughter had undergone a breast enlargement procedure, Timberlake said, 'I don't know about her breasts; I was always too busy looking at her fantastic butt.' He has made some other curious remarks about Britney, including a rather mixed message when, according to biographer Sean Smith, he said, 'That's the greatest thing about Britney; even when she doesn't understand, she understands that she doesn't understand because she has a big heart.' Was he being complimentary or condescending? It's a matter of perspective.

For Britney, her time in Los Angeles with Justin had been quite an eye-opener, for life in the show-business city only added to the pressure she already felt on herself. 'Southern girls can be very hard on themselves because you are expected to act in a certain way, you are expected to please people,' she said. 'And then I moved to Los Angeles when I was very young. I was so under scrutiny. If a hair was out of place, I'd be so anxious. I would get very anxious about so many things.'

Some spoke of Britney back in those days as a sharp, focused, sassy operator, keen to get to the top as fast as her dancing feet could take her. Others remembered her more as a naïve, wholesome girl who didn't quite understand what was going on around her. In another of the dichotomies that would dominate her image, both of these assessments had lots of truth to them. Britney was focused and smart, yet pliable and exploited. She was a sexy star and a southern saint. Her wrestling with these contradictions was to continue for some time before she, and the world, could work out who Britney was. She was also on the way to the top, with her first album set to cement her popularity.

However, for the family, Britney's rise to fame was already proving problematic. In her memoir, Jamie Lynn remembered that 'as deals were made, the family dynamics shifted', because Britney's dream 'was going to affect all of us'. She continued, 'Everyone made sure her needs were met, and we all became responsible for helping her as she reached a greater level of success. We needed to keep her happy and productive.' Things began to change, she wrote. She had always been expected to do what she was told, but now she was taught to defer to Britney all the time. She was told that surely she wouldn't want to do anything that would upset her big sister.

'What complicated things even more was that Momma revelled in the attention that came with being Britney's mother. People were more interested in who she was than ever before, and I think she loved that part of it.' The extraordinary fame that Britney acquired in the years ahead was set to cause friction in the family.

Chapter Four

LIKE A VIRGIN?

Britney was rising fast. The period between nervously recording a demo song for Larry Rudolph and her debut album reaching number one on the US charts was just eighteen months. It was a strong debut. When an album opens with a track as instantly recognizable as '... Baby One More Time', listeners know they are either in for a frontloaded collection which never quite lives up to its opening number, or one that has enough quality to open with its strongest song. Few pop songs, and fewer pop albums, open with such familiar chords as this. It would clearly be the track that would attract most punters to buy the album, so the title song was a fitting choice for opener.

With such a successful standout opening the collection, many listeners would be highly curious as the second track kicked in. Written and produced by Max Martin, Per Magnusson and David Kreuger, '(You Drive Me) Crazy' is anthemic and as close as anyone could expect Britney to get to '... Baby One More Time' at this stage. True feel-good stuff, its use of streamlined rock guitar boosts it considerably. Rarely was the tummy-fluttering excitement of young love as accurately rendered in the 1990s.

'Sometimes', which comes next, is gentler and more

wistful. Britney's voice is more natural here, as she sings along cutely to the slow groove. She pleads for patience and trust from a would-be lover. The key change in the final section gives this a cinematic, summery feel. It is not as memorable as the first two tracks, but it is a welcome respite from their intensity. One reviewer commented that the first three tracks are all about guys: 'Like, she never stops thinking about them.' Well, there's plenty more where that came from.

The style and vibe changes again with 'Soda Pop'. This song combines bubble-gum pop and reggae. It has been dismissed as overly cheesy by some, but Britney was a teenage girl recording an album for other teenage girls – this was not a bid for approval from broad-waisted, beard-scratching prog-rock fans; her followers wanted fun songs about boys.

At first, Britney was concerned about the lyrics and theme of 'Born to Make You Happy'. The overtones of a girl being born to make her lover happy were worrying enough for her to push the song through a couple of rewrites before it felt appropriate. 'I asked them to change the words to "Born to Make You Happy". It was a sexual song,' she told *Rolling Stone*. 'I said, "This may be a little old for me. Because of the image thing, I don't want to go over the top. If I come out being Miss Prima Donna, that wouldn't be smart. I want to have a place to grow."' Whether it was song titles, song lyrics or magazine cover shoots, it seemed that Britney could not quite escape mixed messages in her early years. It's almost as if it was being done on purpose to tease the public. Well, it worked for the label.

In the end, the lyrics came across to most listeners as the cries of a girl who knew things had gone wrong with her partner but didn't know why – a universal and more wholesome theme. However, everyone's a critic, and one described the track's lyrics as 'limp and pathetic'.

Boys are still the theme on the next track – 'From the Bottom of My Broken Heart'. Recorded at 4MW East Studios in New Jersey and at Battery Studios in New York City, the soulful ballad is breezy, slow and sad. Described as everything from 'fluff' to 'cheesy' to 'ace' by critics, it is a long track for a teenage pop album, clocking in at four and a half minutes.

If the next song, 'I Will Be There', sounded familiar, it's because its guitar riff is similar to the one in Natalie Imbruglia's signature hit 'Torn'. The mood is upbeat again, which lifts the energy once more after the previous diversion into heartbreak. Having heard Britney's promises to always be there for the person she is singing to, many listeners would want her as their girlfriend or best friend.

'I Will Still Love You' features strong co-vocals from Don Philip. 'Deep In My Heart' brings to life perfectly the sweetness of a teenage romance where the pair instantly believe they have found their life partner. 'Thinkin' About You' ploughs much the same territory, with Britney singing that her friends are complaining that she spends too much time with her boyfriend and that even when she's not with him she is thinking about him. For her, this 'feels so right', though.

More grown-up, musically at least, is 'E-Mail My Heart'.

It is a more sensitive piano ballad, with the technology theme bringing it up to date. You would not have had lyrics such as 'E-mail me back/And say our love will stay alive' in the 1960s, but other aspects of the song would have sat well back then.

In fact, it was that very decade when the album's closing track, 'The Beat Goes On', was written and composed by Sonny Bono, to be recorded by Sonny & Cher in 1967. It is a moody end to the album. The maturity of it, particularly in comparison to the bubble-gum pop that had preceded it, hinted that there was more to come from Britney, more beats to come, and that they would be of a more mature bent.

On the original pressings of the album, this moody ending was tainted slightly by a hidden spoken message from Britney, in which she thanked fans and promoted the then upcoming Backstreet Boys album *Millennium*, with samples of songs featured on the album.

However, even this cynical add-on could not ruin the mood of Britney's debut. She was so excited and proud as it finally hit shelves on 12 January 1999. Artists frequently say that the day their first album goes on sale is one of indescribable pride. For teenage artists, this feeling can often be multiplied.

It was time to await the reviews. For Britney and for the critics, this was a new experience: she had never been reviewed before, and they had never reviewed her before. Write-ups of debut albums are often cagey affairs, because critics have little yardstick to know how the artist connects with the public and there are no previous albums to measure the current one against. The writers don't know how to aim.

Rolling Stone praised the album for 'effectively transforming this ex-Mouseketeer born in a tiny Louisiana town into a growling jailbait dynamo' but felt that 'the ballads of her debut evoke the worst of Debbie Gibson'. Barry Walters also felt that 'shameless schlock slowies, like "E-Mail My Heart" are pure spam'. AllMusic also claimed a comparison with Gibson. Writing that the album 'sounded as if it could have been cut in 1989, not 1999', Stephen Thomas Erlewine said it 'has the same blend of infectious, rap-inflected dance pop and smooth balladry that propelled the New Kids and Debbie Gibson'. Awarding Britney's debut four out of five stars, he loved its 'catchy hooks, endearing melodies, and engaging Euro-dance rhythms'. Although he felt it had 'its share of well-crafted filler', it was 'a pretty great piece of fluff'.

MTV said that Britney had 'gone back to her school days', adding that 'I expected there to be a lot of filler (there sort of is), though I didn't expect it to be as odd (at least sonically) as it ended up being'. *NME* gave probably the most hostile reception to the album, describing it as 'kindergarten cutsiepie cack'. The cynical, sassy indie weekly was never going to have been top of the list of Britney fans. 'Hopefully,' it added, 'if she starts to live the wretched life that we all eventually do, her voice will show the scars, she'll stop looking so f**king smug, she'll find solace in drugs and we'll be all the more happier for it. Now grow up, girl. Quick!' The more commercially savvy *Billboard*'s Paul Verna considered the album 'a top forty-ready workout filled with hook-laden songs from the same bag as the title cut'.

The album was indeed a success around the world. It came out of the traps quickly, ultimately selling over 10.6 million copies in the US to date, making it the seventeenth bestselling album since 1991. Britney also overtook Alanis Morissette as the youngest artist ever to receive diamond status for an album in the US. It was top of the charts in five territories and in the top ten in seventeen countries. And Britney made history when she became just the fifth artist under the age of eighteen to top the *Billboard* 200. Globally, it sold over 25 million copies.

So, Britney was buzzing as she sat atop the charts – but within months she was experiencing the first major public controversy of her career. It came when she posed for a cover shoot for *Rolling Stone* magazine. The chosen image showed her lying on a pink satin sheet, her white shirt falling open to reveal a black push-up bra and skimpy polka-dot briefs. In her left hand is a phone and in her right a Teletubbies toy. The combination of sexual imagery and a childhood toy were enough to ignite controversy and much more besides. That balancing act between her wholesome, holy southern girl image and that of a sexualized being had tipped firmly in one direction.

You didn't need to be cynical to read between the lines of that cover image. David LaChapelle, a photographer better known for his nude portraits, had taken the shot. One of his images inside the magazine depicted Britney with a child's bicycle, and 'baby' embroidered on the back of her shorts. In case anyone had missed the point being made in the photos, journalist Steven Daly showed them with his accompanying text, which described her as 'jailbait'. He wrote of Britney's 'honeyed thigh' and 'ample chest', as well as her shorts, which cling 'snugly to her hips'.

That issue broke circulation records and caused chatter that was probably record-breaking, too. A church group remarked that she 'pulls no punches when it comes to talking about her Baptist faith', but her 'verbalized commitment doesn't mesh with the sexual messages of her visual image'. She was referred to across the media as a 'vampish seductress' and 'Louisiana's Lolita'. In Scotland, a spokesman for the Catholic Church said, 'People like Britney [should] not be allowed to be role models.' The *Guardian* said she was already showing herself to be an 'astute marketing woman'. The American Family Association described Britney as 'a disturbing mix of childhood innocence and adult sexuality'.

What did Britney herself make of the controversy? Initially, her response was combative. 'What's the big deal?' she asked. 'I have strong morals ... I'd do it again. I thought the pictures were fine. And I was tired of being compared to Debbie Gibson and all of this bubble-gum pop all the time.'

However, she has also since suggested she had mixed feelings over the shoot. 'I don't want to be part of someone's Lolita thing,' she has said, adding that 'it freaks me out' that older men would be lusting after her. She also expressed frustration at the amount of attention that was being lavished on the story. Later, in a subsequent interview with *Rolling Stone*, she suggested that she was just playing a part.

'It's like on TV, if you see Jennifer Love Hewitt or Sarah Michelle Gellar kill someone, do you think that means they go out and do that? Of course not.'

LaChapelle suggested that Britney was in on it all along. 'She got it,' he said. 'She knew it would get people talking and excited.' However, in 2003 she said that she felt like she was 'tricked' by the photographer and that she 'didn't really know what the hell [she] was doing'. Speaking to GQ, she said, 'I was back in my bedroom, and I had my little sweater on and he was like, "Undo your sweater a little bit more." The whole thing was about me being into dolls and in my naïve mind I was like, "Here are my dolls!" and now I look back and I'm like, "Oh my gosh, what the hell?"'

Indeed, her mother has suggested that the family were a little naïve as to what was going on during the two-day shoot. Hundreds of images were taken in and around the Spears household, with family members supervising. Lynne wrote that LaChapelle was an 'eccentric, artsy guy'. However, when it came to the photography in Britney's bedroom, her parents and manager were asked to wait outside, and they only belatedly realized what was happening. Lynne demanded that the photoshoot stop right away while Jamie stormed off.

The thing was, neither worried that the scene they had witnessed in the bedroom would ever see the light of day. They assumed they would be given a veto on which images were used and that the magazine would approach them to offer such approval. Agreements like that are commonplace for celebrity photoshoots, but no such deal was in place this time. When the magazine was eventually published, Lynne reportedly complained that 'things went much further than we realized'.

A deeper naïvety on Lynne's part can be found in the fact that, even as deep into Britney's career as 2008, in her memoir *Through the Storm* her mother wrote that 'despite that magazine cover – or maybe because of it – Britney's career exploded'. The use of the word 'despite' here, even with the qualifying clause, suggested that, even nearly a decade on, Lynne had not quite wrapped her head around what was going on with the photoshoot that day.

The *Rolling Stone* cover is crucial to understanding how Britney's image was shaped and is also a fascinating social document in itself. In 2022, a similar photoshoot of a pop princess would still attract attention but draw little fuss, as seen through the experience of Miley Cyrus, who draws no ire for her racy shoots. However, for Britney the effect was explosive. It jettisoned her into the public eye, boosting her career and tossing her into the blaze of her first public controversy. It is still spoken of to this day in articles and documentaries about her career.

Another sign of how sexualized her image was becoming was how obsessed the media became over the question of virginity. When she was eighteen, she told the world that she was a virgin. The conservative values of her Southern Baptist background were at work here. In a survey, some 66 per cent of Southern Baptists said they thought that abortion should be illegal in all or most cases. What's more, some 63 per cent agreed that 'homosexuality should be discouraged by society'. Given that Britney has long courted her gay followers, this was another contradiction.

In a more wholesome development, in 2001 Britney and Lynne published a novel together called *A Mother's Gift*. The storyline concerns a fourteen-year-old girl named Holly Faye Lovell from a tiny, rural town called Biscay in the US state of Mississippi. She leaves the small southern town where she lives with her mother, a seamstress, in order to pursue her dream of a singing career, not knowing the whole truth about her humble beginnings. The *Guardian* was a bit catty about the book, saying that 'the queen of saccharine proves once again that love and a multi-million-pound marketing campaign really can conquer all'.

Britney needed her mum's heart when rehearsals for her second single to be lifted from the album, 'Sometimes', went wrong. While she was practising for the promotional video, Britney was performing one of her high kicks when she felt something go pop in her knee. 'I was in a lot of pain and I knew something was very, very wrong,' she wrote in *Heart to Heart*. She quickly became hysterical, by her own admission. The crew tried to reassure her that just a bit of ice on the injury would sort the problem out, but she knew her body and could tell this was more serious than that.

Lynne and Rudolph arranged an appointment for her, but the doctor said she just had to calm down and rest her leg. She got a second opinion from a doctor in New Orleans. He X-rayed her leg and gave her the verdict: 'You need surgery as soon as possible. You have a piece of bone floating around your knee.' Britney's career was just starting to take off and now she had a serious injury. The timing was terrible.

For eight excruciating weeks, Britney had to endure the twin challenges of long periods of boring rest and gruelling physiotherapy. The therapists would stretch her leg out and bend it to test how well it was recovering. It was painful, and Britney cried a lot. However, the true 'torture' of this period was the long periods when she had to lie still between appointments. During those long hours that never seemed to end, her mind would travel to dark places. She wondered if her career was over. Just weeks before, she had been flying high; now she was shipwrecked with just her own thoughts for company. She cried onto her mum's shoulder and, somehow, this long, agonizing period eventually came to an end.

Writing in *Heart to Heart*, Britney said she took a lesson from it: 'The Lord and your mind can sometimes have the power to heal you, if you believe you will get better that's half the fight right there.' These words seemed to be a world away from the girl who posed so skimpily for *Rolling Stone*, yet they came just months after the magazine hit the newsstands. Britney was still firmly wrestling with her identity.

Once she had emerged from her injury, Britney looked like she was enjoying herself. In May 1999, she wore a black wig to resemble Cher as she performed the famous singer's hit 'The Beat Goes On' at the World Music Awards in Monte Carlo. Within months, she was performing at the Grammy Awards, where she sang 'From the Bottom of My Broken Heart' and '… Baby One More Time'. Although she failed to win either of the awards she was nominated for, she won plenty of hearts.

When she hosted *Saturday Night Live*, she had a laugh at her own expense by appearing with a huge, obviously false bust. She also guest-starred in an episode of *Sabrina the Teenage Witch*. 'No Place Like Home' was broadcast in September 1999, the first of season four, and saw Sabrina celebrate her eighteenth birthday, deciding to move to Paris for a fresh start. Over in the French capital, Britney appeared for a one-to-one performance of '(You Drive Me) Crazy'. She also taught Sabrina some dance moves and told her that always being surrounded by loads of people 'is sometimes the loneliest place to be'. Melissa Joan Hart, who plays Sabrina, returned the favour by making a cameo in the music video for the song.

Hart remembered fun times with Britney. 'She was young and I could see the stress on her face,' she told the *Bethenny* show. 'I was like, "Do you want to go to lunch?" and she was like, "Yes, yes. Let's go to lunch," and then someone behind her would go, "No, no, no. You have interviews, you have to go to vocal coaching, you have to go to the gym and then you have to go on your tour." And she was like, "Okay, maybe later." And I was like, "Let's go to dinner tonight."'

The star continued,

So I went to her hotel, and I invited her to come out with me and we went to a club. She was underage, so I snuck her in the back door and we did a little dancing, and then people sort of swarmed on top of her and she got stuck at a table hanging out with people, chit-chatting, and I was like, 'I've got to go to work tomorrow, can I go?' And she was like, 'Yeah, yeah, yeah. No, go, I am good. They will get me home.'

Fun times, but an incident around this time woke the family up to the downside of Britney's rocketing fame. One day, Lynne and Jamie Lynn were at home when they heard a 'pounding' on the front door. When they peeped through a curtain to see who was there, they saw a strange man yelling, 'Let me in!' Lynne locked herself and Jamie Lynn in the bathroom with a phone and a gun. They called the police and the man was taken away.

Soon afterwards, the family hired a bodyguard, called Big Rob, to look after Britney. They also got two pedigree German Shepherd dogs to beef up security further. 'We flew out to California to meet the dogs, Rob and Ory, to make sure we were all compatible,' wrote Jamie Lynn. 'They were the best, most loyal dogs, and I think they would have killed to protect us.'

Another time, a stalker was living in a collapsed barn directly outside the family home. He insisted he was married to Britney, and he would cut open tin cans of food with a knife, an alarming anecdote for the family. He was eventually arrested, but the worry was not over because while in custody he told the police he had planted a bomb in the family's house. A bomb squad was dispatched to conduct a major search, but no explosives were found.

There were countless episodes like these, some more serious than others. Strangers would approach the house, and people would walk right up to the property to try to get a peek inside Britney's bedroom. There was a great deal for Britney and her family to come to terms with. In her memoir, Lynne remembered the first time she saw her daughter perform live. She was sitting alongside the stage with the sound team and had a feeling of 'nervousness mingled with excitement and speechlessness'. She continued, 'I watched in awe as Britney sang and danced through her first headlining show. When it was over, I burst into tears, the culmination of an emotionally charged experience capping off years of investment on all our parts to get Britney to this point.'

The level of Britney's fame was put on full display in June 2000, when Kentwood Museum announced an exhibit devoted to her. It included a replica of her childhood bedroom, complete with dolls and bears. The project was conceived by Sandy Reed and Kathy Bryan, respectively a resident and local councilwoman of Kentwood, and involved a complete wing of the museum being given over to Britney, who was then just nineteen years old. According to reports, her parents have donated some her childhood dresses.

However, not everyone in the areas where she grew up are fans. There is a certain amount of jealousy, and when author Sean Smith visited McComb, Mississippi, in 2005, a 'surly waitress' told him: 'Britney Spears? Nobody round here likes her.'

Britney's success was something the family could share together, but it was not enough to paper over the cracks developing in her mum and dad's marriage. For Lynne, divorce seemed a 'completely foreign concept', but, she wrote in *Through the Storm*, she eventually 'un-chose' Jamie due to the serious problems they were facing in their marriage.

Even before Britney was born, her mother had filed for divorce from her father. The grounds for the legal filing were given as adultery, as it was claimed that on the evening of Christmas Day, no less, Jamie cheated on his wife. Just days later, Lynne was pushing open the door of a local attorney's office. She was after a custody order over Bryan, $200 a month in child support and an additional $400 a month in alimony. However, within weeks Lynne had backed down, and in March the petition was officially withdrawn.

Decades later, Jamie Lynn has described in her memoir how the rest of the family would tiptoe around her father and keep things from him to prevent him erupting. 'All the effort we put into keeping Daddy from losing his temper made me uneasy,' she wrote.

One tale involved a day when Lynne was teaching Britney, then fifteen, how to drive. Britney was behind the wheel of her mum's treasured four-door black Lexus. At one point, Britney let the car veer into the wrong lane, and Lynne had to grab the wheel to steer it back on track. Fortunately, no one was hurt. But, as Jamie Lynn put it: 'We all knew Daddy would have a fit if he found out Britney was driving' during the incident.

As for Lynne, she wrote of 'cruel words, flung in the heat of the moment, fuelled by alcohol's energy'. She remembered being told she was 'stupid' and 'selfish'. She remembered a 'co-dependent' relationship, dominated by 'blame, guilt and shame'. She said that 'endless disappointments ... chipped away at my heart and spirit'. There were 'only so many pieces' that could break off, she said, 'before there is nothing left of you'.

In *Britney: Inside the Dream*, Steve Dennis described episodes which were more nightmarish than anything. He wrote of 'Dad's hollering, and Mama sat crumpled on the kitchen floor; Dad begging for forgiveness at her feet and Mama giving him yet another second chance'.

In her own book, Jamie Lynn Spears writes that 'Daddy never really stopped drinking', and the periods when he was out of work saw his consumption rise. She writes that tales of him drinking are 'family lore', including one that happened before she was born but which she has had told to her. The family had gathered at Pizza Hut for a birthday celebration; Jamie was late, and he eventually 'came swaggering in, intoxicated', unable to 'string sentences together'.

No wonder that during these years Britney found singing and dancing such havens. She lived in a household where poverty and pain were dominant. Times were chaotic and often scary, but music was a 'place' she could go to for respite. One day, when Britney was eighteen, she sat down with Lynne and talked to her about this. 'Mama,' she said, 'do you want to live like this for the rest of your life?'

Lynne told Jamie she wanted a divorce, and he took it badly. 'Words were said in the heat of anger' was her diplomatic description of the conversation, though she added that he was not surprised. The couple finally divorced in May 2002. Lynne would end up living in a house called Serenity, a $4.5 million mansion built especially for her by her daughter after Britney said, 'Momma, if you leave Daddy, I will buy you a house.' To cheer her mother up further, Britney bought her a $62,000 Lexus car as a Mother's Day treat. Her success was already coming with challenges, but Britney wanted to remember that it also came with major benefits.

Chapter Five

JUSTIN FEVER

I n 2001, Britney and Justin Timberlake were going steady. It had been nearly three years since they were first rumoured to have begun dating. They had become pop's golden couple, and many of their fans assumed they would marry and be happy forever after.

In January, they flew to Rio de Janeiro for the Rock in Rio festival. The event, which was held over seven nights, had a prestigious line up of headliners: Sting, R.E.M., Guns N' Roses, *NSYNC, Iron Maiden, Neil Young and the Red Hot Chili Peppers. Britney appeared on day four, second on the bill behind Justin's *NSYNC. She and Justin stayed for three nights in a suite at the Intercontinental Hotel, where they ordered fried chicken, chips and masses of cola.

This combination of down-to-earth consumption and a plush hotel was symbolic of Britney's approach to touring in those days. Her tour bus had fitted cabinets, leather couches and a highly comfortable bedroom. In her dressing rooms she required scented candles, potted plants and even small trees strewn with fairy lights. She also asked for long couches to recline on. Pop stars often make exotic and diva-ish requests for their 'riders' – the baskets of goodies they demand are waiting for them when they arrive at venues.

However, Britney's were wholesome and everyman: baked chips, fresh white tuna, Altoids mints, French vanilla coffee, Pop-Tarts, Doritos and a vegetable platter.

These homely food products she asked for backstage were mirrored by those she promoted in plain view. In 2000, she did a promotion with *NSYNC for McDonald's, but it wasn't until the following year that she inked her most celebrated deal. In 2001, she starred in her first commercial for Pepsi, having signed a deal worth, it was rumoured, around $8 million.

She later looked back at the four-day shoot, during which she took on various characters. 'We had a couple of different set-ups, and we had one where I was Robert Palmer,' she told *People*. 'We did a remake of "Simply Irresistible", and I had to go through hair and makeup,' she said. 'It took forever because they were turning me into a man!' She remembered that they made her hair 'too big', and she quipped that she ended up looking 'like a girl with a beard'.

W magazine said the ads were 'iconic' and Britney's entire relationship with the soft drink brand has become noteworthy. In a tribute song that hasn't aged well, the boy band Busted sang of Britney that 'Pepsi lets me taste you'. A subsequent ad, aired during the 2004 Super Bowl, saw her co-star with Enrique Iglesias, Beyoncé and P!nk. It opened in Ancient Rome, where the three pop girls appeared as beautiful gladiators, fighting for the entertainment of Iglesias. *W* magazine described it as 'ninety seconds of pure girl power'.

She has promoted a megastore's worth of other brands.

In 1999, she advertised both Polaroid's i-Zone and the Skechers trainer brand. In 2000 came tie-ups, and she was drummed up by Clairol to advertise their Herbal Essences shampoo, as well as by Got Milk? to give dairy a push – an apt product for a girl who grew up surrounded by cows. The message of the latter ad – to grow up – positioned Britney as a grown-up rocker who every kid could become only if they slurped as much milk as possible.

In 2002 came a tie-up with PlayStation, who launched *Britney's Dance Beat*, a game that saw her search for back-up dancers for a forthcoming world tour. The following year, the Italian food chain Sbarro slipped Britney CDs inside the lids of the supersized paper cups at its outlets.

A less well-fated deal came in the form of her tie-up with New York restaurant Nyla. She partnered with celebrity restaurateur Bobby Ochs on Nyla, which is named after the postal abbreviations for New York and Louisiana, her home state. Set in the chic Dylan Hotel on East 41st Street, it promised to be a celebration of everything she loved about Louisiana, all in the heart of New York City, serving Cajun cuisine to tourists and fans of the singer, some of whom turned up in the vain hope that Britney might be present.

However, she 'terminated her relationship' with the New York restaurant within months, citing mismanagement and a 'failure to keep her fully apprised of information relating to the restaurant and its operations', according to a statement from her team. *New York Magazine* reported that Nyla's first manager, Ochs, claimed that the entire business was $350,000 over budget right from the very first night. Then, food critics described its food as 'average'. Britney had heard and seen enough. 'I wish the restaurant and its current ownership continued success,' she said. But it enjoyed no such thing: not long after Britney's exit, Nyla shut permanently, filing for bankruptcy and leaving a $400,000 debt to its creditors.

There would be further commercial deals, but first, she had a new album to release. Having rested for just six days after the end of the ... Baby One More Time tour in September 1999, Britney returned to New York City to begin recording songs for her next album, with the majority of the recording taking place in November. She put in sessions in three New York studios: Avatar Studios, Battery Studios and Electric Lady Studios. She also recorded at studios in Hollywood and Orlando, as well as two sites in Europe: Cheiron Studios, Stockholm, and La Tour-de-Peilz, Switzerland. She worked with a range of producers, including once again with Max Martin, Rami Yacoub, Per Magnusson and David Kreuger.

She did indeed feel the pressure of living up to the success of her debut, as well as the 'difficult second album' syndrome in general. 'It's kind of hard following 10 million, I have to say,' she told MTV News. 'But after listening to the new material and recording it, I'm really confident with it.' She had begun to perform a couple of the newer tracks on her ... Baby One More Time tour, adding 'Oops! ... I Did It Again' to her set, as well as another new song called 'Don't Let Me Be the Last to Know', a ballad that saw her perform on a flying carpet. 'I mean, of course there's some pressure,' she said of the album. 'But in my opinion, [*Oops!*] is a lot better than the first album. It's edgier – it has more of an attitude. It's more me, and I think teenagers will relate to it more.'

Following the opening of her first album, who could have realistically expected Britney to start her second with even more iconic and familiar opening chords? Yet that is exactly what she did with the title track. In 'Oops! … I Did It Again', she sings about toying with a boy's feelings and admits, in such a catchy style, that she is 'not that innocent'. Right there is a statement that the bubble-gum pop of her debut album is ancient history (albeit quite recent ancient history). Musically, it resembles her debut single with tinges of Michael Jackson.

'Stronger' sees her vocal style go deliberately strange again in heavily rhythmic verses before she bursts into a more mainstream style during the breezier choruses. *NME* gave a striking verdict on the track, saying 'there's the deranged helium synth pop of "Stronger" with the huge ABBA chord change in the chorus that sounds scarier and more robotic than the Backstreet Boys'.

The lyrics, protesting that she is 'not your property', and her insistence that she can 'make it on her own' are a telling prediction of her later battle with her father over her conservatorship. Indeed, eerily, many songs from her pre-conservatorship canon seem to somehow foresee what was going to happen to her, as we shall see.

'Don't Go Knockin' on My Door' kicks off with some more freaky Britney vocals. In contrast to the heartbroken and confused Britney of her debut, here we see her defiant, confidently ploughing forward despite a break-up. It is an 'I Will Survive' for a younger crowd. Up next is an unexpected cover – of '(I Can't Get No) Satisfaction' by the Rolling Stones. Recorded with Rodney Jerkins at Pacifique Recording Studios in Hollywood after she attended the 42nd Annual Grammy Awards, the urban take on a rock classic sees Britney at her most breathy and frustrated. It was the first in what became a series of cover versions that saw the young pop star take on big tunes by historic artists. This showed a certain confidence.

'Don't Let Me Be the Last to Know' is more familiarly Britney-esque. Here, she is waiting on her guy to tell her how much he loves her. For many listeners, this more traditional pop tune was a welcome respite from the stomping urbanity of much of the album. It is one of Britney's favourite songs, not only on the album but across her entire career. 'When you hear the song, it's so pure and delicate,' she told MTV News. 'It's just one of those songs that pull you in.'

'What U See (Is What U Get)' is ominous, and in retrospect one can say the same of 'Lucky' – a song about a famous woman who, despite seemingly having it all (the celebrity, the riches, the looks), is empty, lonely and unhappy on the inside. Who could have guessed at this stage quite how uncanny this narrative of a famous person's tears at night would become for Britney?

'One Kiss From You' is a more universally relatable theme – that of the racing heart young love can encounter. 'Where Are You Now' is one of the underrated tracks from Britney's catalogue. It was originally considered for her debut but was held over for the follow-up.

'Can't Make You Love Me' is a Europop song in which Britney sings that none of her success in life can compare to the attention of the guy she has a crush on. 'When Your Eyes Say It' is a cover of a Diane Warren song, while 'Dear Diary' is another of the album's tracks that could have sat on its predecessor. Here, she sings of wanting to be 'so much more than friends' with a boy on the song, which she says is autobiographical.

What a collection it was, and one that would dispel the doubts of many. As for Britney herself, she was proud as punch. 'When I did the first album, I had just turned sixteen. I mean, when I look at the album cover, I'm like, "Oh, my lordy,"' she told MTV. 'I know this next album's going to be totally different – especially [as] the material … is so much more funkier and edgier. And, of course, it's more mature because I've grown as a person too.'

It was released on 3 May 2000, less than eighteen months after her debut album had hit the shelves. Geoff Mayfield, director of *Billboard* charts, said this was 'very smart timing'. He added, 'My philosophy is when you have a young fan base, get 'em while they're hot.' It is a philosophy quite commonplace in the music industry.

'How does a teen phenomenon follow a trend-setting debut that's sold 9-plus million copies in the US alone?' began *Billboard*'s review, framing the essence of the project's entire challenge neatly. It answered its own question by saying it was 'with a little more of the same [and] also mining new ground that leaves the listener pleasantly intrigued'.

As well as getting to the heart of the album, the *Billboard* review also summed up well a reason why Britney was appealing vocally. While she is not 'a vocal acrobat à la colleagues Jessica Simpson and Christina Aguilera', her 'instantly recognizable style' showed that 'she's developing a soulful edge and emotional depth that can't be conjured with a glass-shattering note'. It concluded that *Oops! ...* 'consistently casts Spears as a young woman coming to terms with her inner power'.

Writing for *Rolling Stone*, Rob Sheffield gave the album a 3.5 out of five stars rating, calling it 'fantastic pop cheese' and celebrating that 'under the cheese surface, is complex, fierce and downright scary, making her a true child of rock and roll tradition'. *NME* had slated her debut and Britney herself in their review of ... *Baby One More Time*, but they praised *Oops! ...*, telling readers that 'on the sly, you know you love it'. It said her music 'gets into your brain like ketamine' as 'an all-encompassing, horrendously realized high', meaning that 'in its own sick way, Britney is drug music'. It took as a case in point the title track, which it said was essentially a harder, carbon copy of '... Baby One More Time' because 'you get your fix in a second of the song opening – the taut eighties Michael Jackson riffs, the squeals, the killer chorus, the uplifting middle bit, it's all in there'.

Entertainment Weekly's David Browne gave the album a B rating, writing that it 'reminds us once again that the best new pop can be a blast of cool air in a stifling room', while Lennat Mak of MTV Asia named it 'a brilliant second album', writing that Spears 'is armed with a more mature and seasoned pop star look, stronger and poppier songs, and of course, extensive media exposure'. On the other hand, AV Club said, 'It's no surprise that, like the single that bears its name, *Oops! … I Did It Again* is a joyless bit of redundant, obvious, competent cheese, recycling itself at every turn and soliciting songwriting from such soulless hacks as Diane Warren and assorted Swedes'.

Oops! … became a huge commercial success, debuting at number one in over fifteen countries, including the US, and reaching the top ten in several others. In the United States, it became the fastest selling album by a female artist since records began in 1991, a record which took fifteen years to be surpassed (by Adele's *25*, which sold over 3.38 million copies in its first week of release). It has sold over 20 million copies internationally.

Meanwhile, for every review of her music, there were more reports about Britney's private life and her relationship with Timberlake, which was proving to be the subject of some fascination for the media. On her nineteenth birthday, Timberlake had a special surprise for Britney. He ordered twenty-six dozen roses to decorate her hotel room in Palm Springs, and the petals from another ten were ordered so they could be strewn across the room. A romantic gesture, but speculation had it that Britney also had eyes beyond Timberlake.

Just months earlier, there had been rumours that Britney and none other than Prince William were obsessed with one another. Following reports that the seventeen-year-old royal had a crush on Britney, she sent him a signed copy of her album, together with some photographs of herself. The story ran away with itself: there were even reports that she was buying a manor house near Gloucestershire so she could be near the royal family's Highgrove home.

Appearing on a British chat show hosted by Frank Skinner, Britney was asked about the rumours. 'We exchanged emails for a little bit, and he was supposed to come and see me somewhere, but it didn't work out – so that was it.' William eventually released a statement complaining that he felt 'exploited' by the speculation. It had certainly been a rumour that was more beneficial for Britney than for the young royal.

In June 2001, a rumour swept the showbiz media that Britney and Justin had been in a car crash that had killed her and put him close to death. The rumour panicked fans: Los Angeles police, fire service and hospitals said they were flooded with hundreds of calls from around the world after Dallas radio station KEGL-FM aired a report during its *Extreme Nighttime Radio Show* claiming that an accident had killed Spears and put Timberlake in a coma.

Following the report, the wild west of the internet fanned the flames of the rumour and took it in all sorts of directions. It was claimed that Spears had been speeding at more than 105 miles per hour on the LA freeways and that an empty liquor flask was found at the scene of the accident. However, the entire story, and all its components, were false. A spokeswoman for Britney told *Entertainment Weekly* that there was no crash, that Britney and Justin were both alive and well, and that the team was considering legal action against those spreading the false stories.

Nevertheless, Britney's relationship with Timberlake was breaking down. She went from hinting that the couple would get married 'some time in the future' to being dumped. Timberlake's mother was the first to hint at the problems, telling *People* magazine that the two were 'having problems right now'.

Timberlake was quick to suggest that the break-up happened because Britney had cheated on him. Revealing that his first three girlfriends had all been unfaithful, he said, 'Britney was the third: it was the same with her as with the first girl who broke my heart and the second. They've all gone down the same way.' He added that he still believed that Britney had a 'beautiful heart' but added: 'If I've lost my trust in someone, I don't think it's right for me to be with them.'

Speaking to chat-show host Diane Sawyer, Britney said the split was 'pretty rough' and 'kind of weird'. Asked by Sawyer if Timberlake's claim that she had been unfaithful to him was correct, Britney sat on the fence: 'I'm not technically saying he's wrong, but I'm not technically saying he's right either,' she said. Sawyer also accused Britney of mistreating Timberlake, driving the pop star to tears. The host also claimed that Britney had upset 'a lot of mothers in this country' with her provocative music videos. Many fans claimed Britney was being 'slut shamed'.

Many commentators feel that it was at this point that Britney's life changed. The sunshine began to hide behind clouds. Up until now, she had been in control of her career to a large extent. She had enjoyed significant input into her promotional videos and live shows and had even helped audition background performers. She seemed a wholesome, happy and healthy young pop star, but the heartache of breaking up with Timberlake, and the change in tone from some of the media, took a lot of the fun out of fame for Britney. The happiness and innocence went out of the window for her. From now on, she would appear a less content and more self-destructive star.

She was reportedly stunned by how vicious some of the media coverage of the break-up had been. Commentators are often too fast to pinpoint a single incident in a star's life as the moment when they began to unravel. For Britney, the story is more complicated than a single break-up causing a downward spiral. However, this was certainly a point at which she took a new path – one that, paradoxically, put her more in the spotlight while surrounding her with more darkness.

In the wake of the break-up, Timberlake released a single that was widely interpreted as a dig at Britney. 'Cry Me a River' was a break-up song – something famously not unheard of in the pop arena. However, what most linked it to Britney was the video, which included a doppelgänger for her playing the part of a cheating girlfriend. The character even wore pink sunglasses – a Britney reference that fans did not need to be detectives to notice.

Britney had already been given the heads-up on the video and was even offered the chance to veto its allusion to her. Remembering a conversation with Timberlake, she told *Rolling Stone*: 'He called me up and behind it was, "And by the way, you're in a video that's coming out. Don't worry about it. It's not a big deal."'

Subsequently, she also got a call from his record label. She said they told her she could veto the video if she wanted. 'I had the power to say no to the video. But I didn't, because I thought, "Hey, it's your video."' Perhaps unsurprisingly, she felt less laid back about the matter after she had actually seen the clip. 'I hadn't seen it,' she said of when she had given her approval. 'Then it came out, and I said, "I should've freakin' said no to this sh*t!" I was so like, "Woah. What is going on right now?"'

Even in her hurt over the video, the pro inside Britney was able to recognize its sass. 'I think it looks like such a desperate attempt, personally,' she said, adding that 'it was a great way to sell the record. He's smart. Smart guy.'

The darker side of fame was always visible in Britney's career, as she faced speculation and reporting about her breasts and the question of her virginity from her teenage years. Much of this content has aged badly, suggesting a certain creepiness in the media's fascination with the young star. However, some have suggested that Britney, or her team, encouraged this prurience.

An early signal of her objectification from a young age came when the media became obsessed with a rumour that Britney had undergone a breast enlargement operation. The promotional video for '(You Drive Me) Crazy' seemed to drive the media crazy as it zoomed in on her chest as she danced. People suggested that it had grown significantly since her last major outing.

When it was announced that Britney was undergoing surgery for a knee injury, some wondered whether this story was a cover to allow her to have the cosmetic operation. Even when she was subsequently on MTV with crutches, some stuck by the boob conspiracy.

Reg Jones threw petrol on the flames when he claimed that his ex-girlfriend had been longing for the procedure for years. 'She started talking about getting a boob job when she was sixteen,' he said. 'She believed that she would be a more popular performer if she had the smoking hot body.'

Perhaps the most infamous example of the speculation over Britney's bust came during an interview in 1999, when Dutch TV reporter Ivo Niehe, a middle-aged man, turned to Britney, who was then seventeen, to say, 'There's one subject we didn't discuss. Everyone's talking about it. Well, your breasts.' The shock in the studio is palpable. Britney, looking less than comfortable, responds, 'My breasts?' Niehe then asks her what she thinks about breast implants. Britney replies that she finds it 'sad' that people thought she had undergone breast surgery. 'If you want to do that, that's fine, but I personally wouldn't do that,' she says.

This interview has become infamous since a clip from it was featured in the recent documentary *Framing Britney Spears*. People on social media have written judgementally of the host, suggesting he was completely out of line. However, Niehe has since insisted that he only broached the subject because Britney's management team asked him to do so in order to give her a chance to respond to the speculation. The infamous *Rolling Stone* cover seemed to cast a shadow over her for years, with the media thinking it made lewd discussion of the teenager's body and sex life fair game.

Whatever the truth about the source of this line of questioning, it certainly seems like a different era. The relentless interest in a teenager's body might be repeated in some sectors of the media now, but it would at least be met with strong criticism rather than with the impunity it once hailed. Speaking to *TV Guide*, Britney tried to bring the story to some sort of conclusion. She denied her much-discussed breasts had gone under the surgeon's knife. 'When I first signed with the record label, we took a lot of photos and those were the pictures that got used,' she said. 'I weighed 105 pounds; I weigh 130 now.' A 'growth spurt' was responsible for the changes to her body, she said.

The issue has never quite been dropped by some corners of the media. Even as recently as 2018, a plastic-surgery commentator speculated that Britney may have undergone what they believed would be a second breast enlargement after a video she posted on Instagram got tongues wagging again.

Meanwhile, back in 2001, Britney was almost synonymous with discussion and speculation over the topic of virginity. She was questioned relentlessly about whether or not she was a virgin. Reporters and commentators wrote thousands of words on the matter. In 2000, she told a radio station: 'Yes, I am a virgin. I definitely want to try not to have had sex until I'm married. I just want to wait for this special someone.'

This was not enough to stop conjecture on the question.

If anything, it only made people more fascinated with the teenager's sex life. A mystery businessman contacted her record label and offered £7.5 million to relieve her of her virginity. Britney was naturally appalled. 'It's a disgusting offer,' she said. 'He should go and have a cold shower and leave me alone. It's outrageous how a man like that can offer something which is totally unacceptable.'

Inevitably, the media were becoming less and less forgiving of the clash in Britney's image between the sexualized young woman of her videos and photoshoots, and the god-fearing, clean-living Baptist she also branded herself as. The *Guardian* said that Britney 'swirls her virginity about like a tasselled nipple'. In phrasing that would no doubt be condemned in 2022, its writer Polly Vernon asked whether Britney was 'a surgically enhanced, cock-teasing hussy' or 'a solid, moral, Christian role model, a vast improvement on the Spice Girls, the anti-Madonna, if you like?' In 2000, *People* magazine featured Britney alongside the headline: 'Too sexy too soon?'

At a press conference before an awards bash in Cannes, France, in 2002, a journalist asked, 'Is it true you are still a virgin?' After a pause, Britney said, 'I wish I'd never said anything about being a virgin now.' When she was pressed further, she insisted, 'That's private.'

She told *Us Weekly* that she was finding it hard to remain a virgin. In 2002, following their break-up, Timberlake gave an interview to Barbara Walters of *20/20*, in which he indicated that the couple had indeed enjoyed full sexual relations. He also gave a radio interview in the same year, during which he was asked whether he had 'f**ked' Britney. He laughed and replied, 'Okay, yeah, I did it.' When this interview resurfaced in a 2021 documentary, it had aged badly and both Timberlake and his interviewers were criticized online. In a statement on Instagram, Timberlake said he was 'deeply sorry' and wanted to 'take accountability' for his actions.

In 2003, Britney told *W* magazine that she was no longer a virgin, though she insisted she had only slept with 'one person my whole life'. She added that it 'was two years into my relationship with Justin' that she had sex, because she 'thought he was the one'. She accused her ex of selling her out with his *20/20* interview.

Meanwhile, she also tried to keep some focus on her music and the vast ambitions she had for it. From her start as a relatively homely performer, Britney increasingly wanted to reach for the iconic. One of the earliest examples of this was the MTV Video Music Awards (VMAs) in New York in September 2001. This ceremony has often been the forum for notable performances from female singers: Lady Gaga hung from the ceiling covered in fake blood in 2009, and Madonna vogued in full Marie Antoinette drag in 1990. Britney upstaged them all.

Her performance of 'I'm a Slave 4 U' was jungle-themed from the start. She appeared on the stage of the Metropolitan Opera House in an unforgettable outfit. She wore a green bra top with jewelled pants and brown boots, her navel glittering. However, the most jaw-dropping part of her costume was a live one: a huge amelanistic python. All the celebrities, on stage and in the audience, were competing for public attention, but just like that Britney had made the entire planet sit up and take notice of her.

The snake's handler had happy memories of working with Britney, who he said was nervous of the reptile at first. 'She was very good,' Michael Hano told *Today*. 'She was very focused and initially she was scared of the snake, but you could see that she was able to focus and kind of push yourself to be able to work with the thing and look comfortable doing it.'

Looking back on the snake performance twenty years later, Britney wrote on Instagram: 'I will tell you this ... before I went on that night I was feeling kinda out of body with nerves.' She added, 'Justin saw I could hardly talk so he held my hand and gave me a five-minute pep talk which obviously worked.'

However, the animal rights body PETA was less impressed. In a statement, the group said, 'PETA opposes speciesism, a human-supremacist worldview.' Britney eventually concluded that the episode was not one to be repeated. 'It's insane! Why did I do that? It's so dumb!' she told E! News in 2016. Asked if she was likely to repeat it, she replied, 'Hell no.'

A week after her MTV performance, Britney shared in a moment of perspective that many felt following the September 11 attacks. She was in the air when the attacks were taking place, on a flight headed to Sydney in Australia. She only learned of the attacks when she landed down under. Like many Americans that day, she was quickly on the phone to check that her relatives were okay, particularly her brother, Bryan, who lived in New York.

In the light of the attacks, she cancelled part of her activity in Australia and then shelved commitments in South America and Europe. Keen to help out with the fundraising for the victims, she ruled that $1 from every ticket sold on her next tour should be given to young children who had been bereaved in the 9/11 attacks, a move which raised more than $2 million.

Drawing on her experience on *Sabrina the Teenage Witch*, Britney took a deeper plunge into the world of acting when she starred in teen road movie *Crossroads*. Directed by Tamra Davis from a screenplay written by Shonda Rhimes and based on a concept conceived by Britney herself, the film saw her star alongside Anson Mount, Zoe Saldaña, Taryn Manning, Kim Cattrall and Dan Aykroyd. Describing *Crossroads* as 'my little project', Britney told MTV that she talked to Rhimes and 'told her what I wanted the movie to be about and she elaborated on it'. She added, 'When you do a movie, I think you have to be really passionate about it. I was having a lot of offers, but this is something my heart was into.'

Another film offer had raised an eyebrow for Britney when she noted that Steven Spielberg was involved in the production. The concept was billed as a cross between *The Flamingo Kid* and *Dirty Dancing* and she was thrilled at the prospect, but the movie never got off the ground, so *Crossroads* it was. There, she played opposite the film's hunk, played by Mount, who was encouraged to take the part by Robert De Niro, a fan of Britney's.

Filming on *Crossroads* began in March 2001. The theme was familiar and well-trodden enough: three childhood best friends and a man they just met take a road trip across the country, finding themselves and their friendship in the process. Britney told MTV that it 'is about this journey that the three of us best friends take, finding ourselves and what we want out of life and getting our friendship back'. She added, 'Friends are all you have at the end of the day', and 'when your boyfriend breaks up with you, who do you call – your girlfriend'. She played the film's lead, Lucy. Commenting on her 'perfectionist' character, she said, 'She is very different from me' because she needed everything to be done 'her way', whereas Britney considered herself 'a little bit more ... carefree'. The movie's soundtrack included her song, 'I'm Not a Girl, Not Yet a Woman'.

Director Tamra Davis later spoke with *Variety* about her experiences working with Britney. Davis had previously declined to take part in the film, as she was suspicious of working with celebrities with little experience of acting. However, she was persuaded to meet Britney in the Las Vegas hotel she was staying in. 'I got there in the morning at like 10 a.m. at some big fancy suite, and Brit opened the door and she was like wearing a little T-shirt and underwear and she was like, "Last night, I was hammered!"' said Davis. 'I was like, "Who's this girl?!" She was hilarious and I just thought she was amazing.' Davis said they 'spent the whole day together and she proved to me that she really wanted to do this and put in the work and wanted it and was very serious about it'.

Working with such a superstar brought intense attention to the production of the film. 'We had to hide a lot,' continued Davis. 'People would drive by and honk, or a thousand people would just show up to see Britney. Driving around in a convertible with her might as well have been in a parade.'

The film was largely shot in and near Louisiana, although indoor scenes were often filmed in Los Angeles. The cast and crew used fake names for Britney and 'moved around pretty quickly' to try to protect their star's privacy. 'We just had to keep moving fast and try to ask the fans to please not yell while we were trying to shoot,' she said. Britney was involved in casting and, indeed, almost everything, said Davis. 'I don't think anything happened on the film without making sure Brit was happy with it,' she said.

She found some parts of acting rather challenging, particularly the requirement to cry on demand. 'It's the end of the day, and you're just like, "Man, I can't get that sad. What's with me?"' she recalled. According to reports, there were also topless scenes shot of Britney, but no such scenes have ever seen the light of day.

The crew soon cottoned on that one of the ways to keep her happy was to have Timberlake, who she was still in a relationship with at the time of production, visit her on set. 'Oh yeah, he was around,' said Davis. When she went and knocked on the couple's door in the morning, Davis was mindful of Britney's image at the time: 'So I'd be picking her up in the morning and I'd be like, "I'm not gonna say anything. Don't worry! Those are personal questions!"' However, she added, the couple 'were the most adorable'.

There was a certain degree of pressure on Britney when the film was completed. There is cynicism about pop stars turning actors, not least because of Mariah Carey's notorious movie *Glitter*, which was released the year before and took just $5 million at the box office against a $22 million budget. The diva blamed the 9/11 attacks for the movie's poor commercial showing, as it was released just ten days after the disaster. However, the critics, to put it mildly, felt the real problem was the film's lack of quality. It was nominated as the worst musical of the past twenty-five years, and movie magazine *Fade In* said that 'trotting out every hoary cliché about the music business imaginable, *Glitter* isn't just one of the worst music-themed films ever made – it's one of the worst films ever made, period'.

Upon its release, *Crossroads* divided viewers and critics – the former loved it, while the latter absolutely panned it. It exceeded box office expectations, making more than $61 million on a relatively modest $12 million budget. John Anderson of the *Los Angeles Times* wrote that Britney 'acquits herself as well as anyone might, in a movie as contrived and lazy as this one', while Chris Kaltenbach of the *Baltimore Sun* said, 'Go see *Crossroads* if you want to hear Britney sing or see her wear next-to-nothing. But otherwise, avoid this train wreck at all costs.'

Lisa Schwarzbaum of *Entertainment Weekly* was more

positive, comparing *Crossroads* with other pop stars' forays into cinema and declaring that the movie 'not only makes excellent use of the singer's sweetly coltish acting abilities, but it also promotes a standardized set of sturdy values with none of Mariah Carey's desperate *Glitter*, or any of Mandy Moore's gummy pap in *A Walk to Remember*'.

Jane Crowther of the BBC wrote that 'Spears manages to come across on film as natural, endearing, and extremely likable', while Bret Fetzer remarked that the movie 'could have been trite schmaltz, but the script has some grit and the direction is fresh and relaxed – and, most significantly, Spears is far more sympathetic and engaging than you might expect'.

Robert K. Elder of the *Chicago Tribune* complained that Britney 'delivers a performance with the same sincerity she invests into a Pepsi commercial', while Claudia Puig of *USA Today* considered it 'less a movie than a mind-numbingly dull road trip'. The *Washington Post* said it was 'an extended-play advertisement for the Product that is Britney'. *Time* named it one of the top-ten worst chick flicks.

The film has certainly divided critics.

With the majority of the more negative reviews written by male critics, some have wondered if there was an element of misogyny in the film's reception. Writing for *Harper's Bazaar*, Mekita Rivas pointed out, for example, that Timberlake 'didn't experience nearly the mockery or pushback when he tried to embark on a similar pop star-to-actor path, starring in several film and TV projects'.

Davis said, 'I feel like she was unfairly criticized because we tested the movie like crazy and the audience, especially girls, loved that movie.' She pointed out that the film 'was made for girls' and 'did what it was supposed to do to its audience', adding that 'it's such an easy thing to take a cheap shot at somebody like that. Britney was an easy target for people.'

Girls did indeed love the movie. On its opening day, *Crossroads* grossed an estimated $5.2 million in 2,380 cinemas, becoming the second highest grossing film of the day. On the first weekend of its release, *Crossroads* remained in second, grossing an estimated $14,527,187. Worldwide, the film grossed a total of $61,141,030. Britney was recognized with five nominations across the MTV Movie Awards and the Teen Choice Awards. However, the film also attracted some less favourable gongs, including Most Flatulent Teen-Targeted Movie. She also tied with Madonna for worst actress, with the elder pop queen being (dis)honoured for her part in *Swept Away*, a widely derided movie directed by her husband, Guy Ritchie.

It was not an entirely happy project for Britney. She declined to meet devoted fans who had waited for hours to get autographs and chat to the star at the premiere. Some of the 3,000 fans – who had come from as far away as South Africa, according to reports – booed and hissed her when she was rushed into the screening just moments after arriving at the Odeon Leicester Square in London's West End.

At a recent premiere event, Tom Cruise and Penelope Cruz had hit the headlines when they spent an hour talking to fans, even agreeing to talk to friends and family on fans' mobile phones. Britney, who arrived almost an hour late to the *Crossroads* premiere, was unable to live up to this. The next morning's press included quotes from disappointed fans and their parents who had waited for several hours in the hope of meeting Britney. It would not be the last time she would let down London fans.

Britney also dipped her toe into the world of acting when she made a cameo in the NBC comedy series *Will & Grace*. Rachel Browne of the *Sun-Herald* said of Britney's appearance that 'it's impossible to accept her in any role other than her own headline-hugging self', but the *Sunday Mail* was more upbeat, commenting that she 'does well, especially when you remember the dismal *Crossroads*'.

She also appeared in the CBS comedy series *How I Met Your Mother*. A fan of the show, she asked her team to contact co-creators Carter Bays and Craig Thomas, and despite some misgivings over casting such a huge star she got the role of Abby. The character was a receptionist at a dermatology clinic who unsuccessfully tried to gain the affections and attentions of client and show protagonist Ted. The cast and crew were 'instantly impressed with Spears' comedic acting', wrote Kara Hedash. The series enjoyed a bump in ratings.

Britney came under criticism again when she was accused of raising a finger to fans in Mexico. She was caught on camera with an extended middle finger as she left the airport in Toluca, outside Mexico City. She had to perform some damage control – and fast. 'I'm human too. I get mad like everyone else,' Reuters quoted her as saying. She insisted that the targets of her gesture were the paparazzi, who she said were driving recklessly around her car and nearly caused a collision. The finger was not for her Mexican fans, who she said 'are so amazing'.

A documentary shot during the tour showed how stressed and under pressure Britney felt. She was rushed from one promotional commitment to another and kept saying that she hoped to take a vacation in Mexico City or Greece once the tour dates and other commitments were over.

A press conference got uncomfortable when a journalist asked her to stand up so he could see the outfit she was wearing. She obliged, sparking wolf-whistles from some in the room. The reporter then asked her to turn around so he could see her backside. At this, she drew the line. She quickly sat back down and told the reporter, 'You can see when I leave.'

Her second concert at Mexico City's Foro Sol Stadium saw her performing for 52,000 fans. During the fifth song, 'Stronger', she abruptly left the stage, saying only, 'I'm sorry, Mexico. I love you. Bye,' according to reports. An announcement came over the PA telling fans to go home. Some shouted 'Fraud! Fraud!'

The following day, concert promoters issued a statement blaming the cancellation on safety concerns caused by a thunderstorm. It quoted Britney as saying, 'The Mexican fans are some of the best in the world. However, for the security of my company and the audience, as well as for the show's quality, I had to suspend my performance.'

It had not been a successful tour. Judy Hoffman, who made the documentary, emerged feeling sadness and empathy for Britney. 'You just felt her loneliness and sadness, and it was hard to talk to her,' Hoffman told *Vanity Fair*. 'I just wanted to leave her alone. I felt so sad. I didn't want to be another press person torturing her. I just didn't want to be like the people I saw that she had to encounter all the time.'

However, the mixed experience she had with *Crossroads* and in Mexico were mere sideshows compared to her overall level of popularity at this stage. Put simply, everything was blowing up and the world was falling apart for Britney. She was named the world's most powerful celebrity by *Forbes* magazine in June 2002, beating off the likes of Madonna, U2 and Tiger Woods. As she approached her third album, Britney had gone further than she could ever have dreamed. She had already learned that the journey towards superstardom involved some rocky terrain. But in terms of the joy of public adoration and the unpleasantness that can come with it, Britney hadn't seen anything yet.

When you listen to some of the lyrics on Britney's early albums, you could be left wondering if she had a crystal ball. Her third, *Britney*, saw her develop a more mature sound and more grown-up lyrics. Whereas her first two albums had hinted at adult themes, here the top-shelf talk was more explicit, in the shape of topics such as coming of age, control, manipulation and sexuality. How pertinent some of these themes would be for her further down the line.

Explaining the more mature approach she was aiming for, Britney said she wanted an 'older generation to pick up on' the new album. To this aim, she did fairly well. Musically, the range of genres she touched on was the broadest to date. As well as straightforward pop, there were slices of disco, electronic dance, reggae, hip-hop, rock and electronica.

The fact she named the album simply *Britney* felt like a statement in itself. She was telling the world that this album, more than its predecessors, revealed the real Britney. Mindful that some saw her as a pop puppet who merely fronted a creative operation dominated by others, she wanted to shake things up. She was certainly more involved in its creation – she co-wrote six of the tracks.

For her, the success of the album was not to be based only on sales and verdicts; the person she was trying harder than ever to impress was herself. 'This is the first album I have ever really written and taken my time on, so when I actually listen to the whole album, it's just that much more special,' she told MTV News. 'I don't know if I'm the best songwriter in the world, but I had a lot of fun doing it and hopefully I will get better and grow.'

The size of the team she assembled for the album reflected the scale of her ambition. She worked with a vast and impressive team of people, including Pharrell Williams' songwriting duo The Neptunes. 'I was inspired by a lot of hip-hop and R&B while I was on my last tour,' she said. 'I was inspired by Jay-Z and The Neptunes.' She said she wanted them to help her make the album 'nastier and funkier'.

Again, she nails it with an iconic opening track. 'I'm a Slave 4 U' strides right across the bridge that previously connected her pop essence with her R&B aspirations. Naturally, the song's title and theme were often remarked upon during the campaign to free Britney of her conservatorship. The crystal ball seemed to be earning its keep.

Dance pop 'Overprotected' also carried some ironic resonance during the guardianship years. A song about a girl who is tired of being coddled and just wants to be herself, the melody moves this way and that, hinting at a number of genres as it goes. She questions what she will do with her life and how she is supposed to know what's right. She adds that whenever she tries to state her own thoughts and feelings, she stands corrected. Vocally, she did a magnificent job here. *Entertainment Weekly* said her voice 'hovers between testiness and aggression'.

'Lonely' is about a girl moving on from a troublesome romance after being lied to and manipulated. She is livid that someone thought she was so naïve that she could be played with. Rarely has the confusion and challenge of adolescence been so accurately rendered.

The fourth track has become one of her best-known songs: 'I'm Not a Girl, Not Yet a Woman'. Again, the prescient themes can be felt as she sings that there is no need to protect her. 'It's really where I'm at right now and something I can really relate to,' she told MTV News of the song. She sings about being tired of being judged and protected by those around her. Britney expresses a yearning to make her own choices and decisions as she develops into womanhood. At the time, the song came across as one that deals with the universal experiences of people as they grow up, and it still does, but it also presages the curious path Britney was to find herself on in the future.

'Boys' is forgettable and was dismissed by one reviewer as 'cut-rate eighties Janet Jackson'. That said, her closing sentiment – 'can't live with 'em, can't live without 'em' – would be only too relatable for her listeners. 'Anticipating' is not about boys – it's about friendship between girls. Many reviewers considered it the strongest track on the album, because it offered fans something a bit different melodically as well as thematically, a respite from the wall-to-wall theme of boys and romance elsewhere in her works.

In 'Cinderella', Britney is the girl who moved on from her boyfriend after he failed to appreciate her efforts in the relationship. In 'Let Me Be' she asks, 'Won't you just let me, let me be?' and assures that she can stand on her own. 'Bombastic Love' and 'That's Where You Take Me' are both about happier times; in the former she predicts a relationship that will be just like in the movies, and in the latter she sings about how safe her heart feels. 'When I Found You' sees her sing that she has found her 'deepest love' in her soulmate, who is essentially a reflection of herself. 'What It's Like to Be Me' is a yearning for curiosity and empathy from any man who wants to make her their own.

Britney was first released in Japan on 31 October 2001, followed by releases in Europe, North America and beyond.

Britney said again that she hoped this album would make a statement that she was developing as an artist. 'I couldn't do ... *Baby One More Time* number three,' she said on the eve of its release. 'I had to change it up and pray people think that's cool.'

In the reviews, there was a sense of backlash. For instance, *Entertainment Weekly* dismissed her 'virginal vamping in an awkward adolescence' and 'a few tentative new moves'. On PopMatters, Nikki Tranter wrote that 'many of the tunes are good for a romp around the kitchen (or the dance floor, if you prefer) but the girl is right when she says she is yet to come into her own both as a woman and a recording artist'.

Rolling Stone gave it 2.5 stars out of five, hinting that they found the album a little inward-facing. Barry Walters wrote that she is 'now so high-concept, such a distillation of what made pop singers like Paula Abdul, Janet Jackson and Madonna so fabulously marketable, that her third record, *Britney*, is a concept album about herself'. Taking a tone some would find inappropriate, Sal Cinquemani of *Slant* magazine said, 'It's time for Spears to quit being such a cock-tease and cook something up that will satisfy the ever-vacillating hype-machine.'

He complained that her 'Lolita shtick is nearly past its expiration date, and the growing pains presented throughout the album too often come across as contrived'. Surprisingly, he even raised the recent September 11 attacks, writing that 'America itself has aged abruptly over the past two months' and it remained to be seen whether 'any of her incarnations remain relevant in an era that's suddenly not that innocent'.

Billboard was more positive, saying the album was a 'nicely varied, wholly satisfying collection' that 'shows Spears taking solid first steps as a songwriter, as she deftly explores the emotional fallout and eventual empowerment of growing up under a public microscope'.

Britney debuted at number one on the US *Billboard* 200, enjoying first-week sales of 745,750 copies. This was the second highest first-week sales by a female artist behind her own previous album, *Oops! ...* She also became the first woman to have her first three studio albums debut at the top of the US charts. She sold over 5 million copies in the US and 9 million worldwide. It was clear that the public was listening to Britney's songs more than the critics' words.

To support the album, she embarked on the Dream Within a Dream tour. Over nine months, she performed sixty-nine shows. The choreography, devised by Wade Robson, aimed to evoke her coming of age and new-found independence. The show was divided into seven segments including the encore and saw everything from her hanging from a gyrating wheel to jumping in bungee cords onto the stage and dancing in a mocked-up jungle.

Most memorably for many, during the encore there was a water screen that pumped 2 tons of water into the stage. 'I've read reviews that compared it to the candelabra in *Phantom* or the helicopter in *Miss Saigon*,' said one of the team behind the water feature. Also relevant is that the set list leant so heavily on her current album. Such a bias is usual to a degree on a tour, but with her older hits dealt with during a brief medley, the feeling that Britney was trying to seize control of her sound in favour of one that she felt reflected her better was palpable.

The *National Enquirer* said that the concert 'packed more technical wizardry than *Harry Potter*, but almost no actual singing'. However, the *San Francisco Chronicle* felt the show 'was pure Britney excess' and 'hugely entertaining'. The tour was a big earner, taking $56.8 million at the box office – it seemed Britney was unstoppable.

Chapter Six

WHAT HAPPENED IN VEGAS

B ritney knows how to kick up a storm and get herself on the front pages. These moments often come at music awards evenings, and at the 2003 MTV VMAs she enjoyed a prolonged kiss with Madonna during their opening performance for the ceremony. The world went crazy.

Britney opened the show with a nod to pop history by singing Madonna's 'Like a Virgin', emerging out of a wedding cake while dressed as a bride, as Madonna did in her 1984 VMAs performance. Christina Aguilera joined Britney on stage before Madonna appeared and launched into her single 'Hollywood'. During the performance, Madonna leaned over and kissed Spears, sending shockwaves through the area and far beyond.

For Britney, who had become quite the fan of Madonna (a hero-worship that began when she was a child), this was the culmination of years of devoted interest in the pop star. 'I remember being eight or nine years old, running around my living room singing and dancing and wanting so much to be like her,' she wrote in *Rolling Stone* in 2010. 'All my girlfriends still listen to her stuff. We're all mesmerized by her. Madonna's stage presence has inspired so many artists. You can see her influence in the recent generations of artists who have picked up some of her moves and have been influenced by her style.'

In the run-up to her live shows, Britney would blast out one of the singer's albums in her dressing room, usually *Ray of Light* or *Music*. Then, soon before stage time, she would gather her team for a prayer circle and pre-show motivational huddle, a technique Madonna had long been famous for employing herself.

She remembered the first time she met Madonna. 'The first time I met her was when I flew to visit her at one of her shows in 2001,' she wrote. 'I walked into her dressing room, and her daughter, Lola, was there, and I felt really nervous.' Spears told Madonna: 'I feel like I should hug you.' Looking back, she squirmed at the memory. 'I was so stupid! But she was so nice about it. I would definitely not be here, doing what I'm doing, if it wasn't for Madonna.'

At the VMAs, she got more than a hug and was delighted by the reaction it caused. Her ex-boyfriend, Timberlake, was in the audience and looked gobsmacked. The world's media went wild. Britney decided that she and her hero were now 'soulmates' and even quipped that perhaps Madonna was her husband in a different life.

Britney would lean into her friendship with Madonna to guide her own career, as she later admitted during a chat with *Harper's Bazaar*. 'I guess she's really taught me to stay true to myself,' she said. 'That seems like a simple thing to say, but she taught me through action, not just by saying it. There are so many people around you that have opinions but, but you just have to listen to your instincts.'

As for Madonna, she said that Britney has 'a certain fragility' and 'vulnerability' that 'makes me feel maternal towards her'. She added that she recognized some of herself in Britney, noting that the young singer was forever in a tricky situation, where when 'you make a mistake, the whole world is watching [and] they beat up on you'.

It was through Madonna that Britney first heard about Kabbalah. This branch of Jewish mysticism has been seized upon by celebrities in the US, particularly on the West Coast, where a modernized, simplified version has taken hold. Madonna gave Britney copies of the Zohar, the central text of Kabbalah, which offers a mystical commentary on the books of the Jewish bible, the Torah. Although the text of the Zohar is in Aramaic, Madonna said the words were so powerful that merely to meditate on their shapes would prove a powerful spiritual experience.

Britney fell hard for Kabbalah, even getting the Hebrew words 'Mem Hey Shin' – a meditation using the holy name to bring healing – tattooed on her neck. 'Kabbalah has helped my soul,' she told *Elle* magazine. 'I was brought up a Baptist ... everything's in codes. The thing that drew me to Kabbalah is, it all comes from light. This sounds so weird, I know, but ... it all stems from light.'

It had been quite the spiritual journey for Britney, from her Southern Baptist roots to this very modern take on a very ancient belief system. Along the way, she had also studied a book called *Conversations with God*. Written by Neale Donald Walsch, it covered how the author sent letters to God and received answers to his questions. The book series, which first emerged in 1995, was enormously successful, parking itself on the *New York Times* bestseller list for nearly three years. Speaking on a 2013 documentary, Britney said, 'I believe there's definitely other forces out there other than angels, guardians, protectors. I definitely believe in heaven. I know there is a place beyond our wildest dreams.'

Like some other famous people who have followed religious groups, Britney eventually felt she was being chased for her cash, according to reports. *Today* said she eventually asked for all her Kabbalah paraphernalia to be removed from her property. 'She's tired of the way [Kabbalah figures] kept hassling her for money,' an unnamed source told *People*.

Meanwhile, there was a new album to be made. Britney had planned to take a six-month break but found herself working on the album sooner than planned. The idea for the title, *In the Zone*, came from the term Larry Rudolph first used to describe the place Britney gets into when she is dancing. Britney took up the phrase and ran with it, warning that anyone who tried to interrupt her at such a time was in for bad luck. 'Don't even try to talk to her now, she's in the zone!' she would say of herself. Even with the new album title, it seemed, Britney was telling the world she would not be knocked off what she saw as her track.

'Me Against the Music' saw her sing alongside her long-time hero Madonna. A love letter to simply letting yourself go on the dancefloor, it sees Britney and Madonna trade lines. It felt almost as if Madonna was luring Britney into a more adult, darker region. In a very mixed reaction, *Slant* magazine said it was 'arguably one of Britney's finest moments and one of her mentor's worst'.

The second song, '(I Got That) Boom Boom', is an unexpected turn: an Atlanta-style hip-hop track featuring the Ying Yang Twins. The two artists, who aren't actual twins, open the song with a memorable suggestion, 'We finna go to the club and get crunk with Britney!' 'Showdown' felt more like dancehall, with a sassy delivery to the chorus. A reviewer mentioned its 'bubbly beats'.

'Breathe On Me' was a heroically unsubtle song about oral sex. The lyrics left little room for doubt on what the song was about – 'just put your lips together and blow' – and her erotic breathing took any remaining uncertainty out of the equation. How far she – and us – had come since the innocent songs of her debut. *Glamour* said it was 'the closest Spears has ever come to a Madonna *Erotica* era' and called it 'sex personified, with a bridge that literally builds and explodes like an orgasm'.

In 'Early Mornin'' Britney is looking for men in nightclubs, while 'Touch of My Hand' is about masturbation, as Britney sings that she will 'teach myself to fly' and 'love myself'. There is another meaning here: that she refuses to please others. 'The Hook Up' has a reggae flavour and sees Britney attempt a Jamaican accent, with varying degrees of success.

And 'Shadow' is about the way a partner can linger in the air even after he's left – ironically the track is one of the more forgettable.

Then comes 'Brave New Girl', another song that fitted well with the defiant theme that Britney intended for the collection. Originally named simply 'Brave Girl', this choppy track has electro-funk beats and features Britney singing about finding her passion and 'that special kiss'.

'Everytime' is a beautiful piano-based ballad which sees Britney's breathy vocals plead for forgiveness for accidentally hurting a former lover. Her co-writer for the track, Annet Artani, said the track was written as a response to Justin Timberlake's 'Cry Me a River', but Britney has neither confirmed nor denied. The theme of a lover's influence lingering after he has gone makes this song a twin with 'Shadow'.

That would have been the most memorable, standout track of the album had it not been for the presence of the iconic 'Toxic'. Written and produced by Bloodshy & Avant, with additional writing from Cathy Dennis and Henrik Jonback, it moves Britney into a new terrain: bhangra music. It is one of the most instantly identifiable and addictive songs she has written. For most listeners, this was the song that gave Britney the musical credibility she had sought for so long.

The maturity of the album was reflected by the reviews. Unlike her previous albums, wrote Dorian Lynskey of the *Guardian*, *In the Zone* has 'no filler and no shoddy cover versions, just fifty-seven varieties of blue-chip hit-factory pop'. He enjoyed its 'southern hip-hop, deep house, Neptunes-style R&B, the ubiquitous Diwali beat and, most importantly, oodles of Madonna' and awarded the album four stars out of five.

For Sal Cinquemani of *Slant*, 'for the most part, *In the Zone* is a big, fat, thumping love letter to the dancefloor'. He continued, 'For a girl who's always seemed too sexed-up for her age, *In the Zone* finds Britney finally filling her britches, so-to-speak, [because] her little girl coquettishness actually works now.' Jason King of *Vibe* said it was 'a supremely confident dance record that also illustrates Spears's development as a songwriter'.

There were more negative takes too. 'Throughout the disc, Ms Spears sounds more dazed than zoned, as if making it clear that she's a less-than-willing participant,' said Kelefa Sanneh of *The New York Times*. Sanneh said that singing was not Britney's 'strength' and added, 'The album is almost perversely devoid of personality – a final act of rebellion, perhaps, against the music industry.' *Rolling Stone* magazine said that 'the harder Spears tries to be Madonna or Janet Jackson, the less convincing she is [because] her voice is so processed, its physicality almost disappears'. Joining several critics in describing the albums beats as better than its vocals, Jon Pareles concluded that 'beyond the glittering beats, Spears sounds about as intimate as a blowup doll'.

David Browne of *Entertainment Weekly* said that 'on a CD intended to celebrate her lurch into adulthood, Spears remains distant and submerged. For all her freedom, she's still finding her way.'

The BBC's Ruth Mitchell also leant into the question of Britney's maturity but asked her not to grow up too quickly. 'She should ... place less emphasis on how self-fulfilled she has become, in repeatedly declaring this she simply draws attention to all the growing up she still has to do,' she wrote. 'Don't rush it, girl! Enjoy being young!' So did Mim Udovitch of *Blender*, who wrote, 'This I'm-coming-out record is an unhesitant move from songs of the heart to songs of the groin.'

Commercially, the album made a splash, debuting at the top of the charts in the US, France, Argentina, South Korea and Mexico. That achievement in the US meant she was the first female artist to have four consecutive number-one albums, surpassing the record she had set with her previous outing. It sold half a million copies in the UK and 3 million copies in the US.

The price of fame hit home again for Britney when, in April 2003, her lawyers reached an out-of-court deal and agreed to drop legal action against a Japanese fan who was accused of stalking her. She withdrew a request for a restraining order to keep Masahiko Shizawa, forty-one, of Yokohama, Japan, away from her – despite her having said in court papers that Shizawa sent her hundreds of love letters and photos and followed her to her homes. In legal papers, she said that Shizawa turned up at her houses in Louisiana and Hollywood. She claimed that he wrote 'I'm chasing you' on one of the pictures he sent, while Shizawa maintained that he was only 'an avid fan'. It had been another distraction from what she considered her focus: music.

Meanwhile, also away from the music, Britney was about to embark on her weirdest moment yet. 'What happens in Vegas, stays in Vegas' goes the saying. For Britney, this came true in the strangest circumstances in January 2004, when she visited Sin City and got married. Just fifty-five hours later, an annulment was complete.

The signs that Britney was out of control had been showing themselves in the run-up to the trip. As the family had gathered in Kentwood for Christmas, Britney rolled up with a brand-new Mercedes as a gift for Lynne. However, on Christmas Eve, she and Bryan borrowed the present to go out partying. They came back the next morning 'looking like they had been up all night', by Jamie Lynn's account. Inside, the car was a mess, strewn with rubbish including bottles and even a razor blade. Lynne was not impressed.

Britney's next present was a girls' trip to the Caribbean island of Nevis for the female members of the family. During the trip, Jamie Lynn noticed that Britney was 'secretive' and 'keeping her distance'. She smoked a lot and drank a lot of cocktails. Her little sister also noticed that Britney was starting to look more and more 'dishevelled' and was taking less care over her appearance. 'After years of making me a priority and spending time together, my sister was now moving on without me.'

After the trip, the travelling party landed at a private airport in Hammond on New Year's Eve. However, Britney and her cousin Laura Lynne stayed on the plane, where they were joined by Jason Alexander and some others. Britney had known Alexander since kindergarten; he was a local boy who went on to develop a crush on her. A strapping American football player, he had a big presence. The last thing that her sister said to Britney before they set off was, 'Now don't go and marry Jason while you're there, Britney!' The elder sister rolled her eyes in response, but what prescient words they turned out to be.

Once in Vegas, the group checked into a suite at the Palms Casino Hotel. Alexander was, according to the *Daily Mail*, 'a swaggering heavy drinker who could have been a younger Jamie Spears'. It was New Year's Eve, and Britney was determined to enjoy herself. Leaving the $10,000-a-night suite, she and her friends took to the hotel's nightclub, Rain. She reportedly sank plenty of vodka, gave Alexander a snog and eventually left the bar at 3.30 a.m.

According to a surreal account of the stay that Alexander sold told the British tabloid *News of the World*, he and Britney had been watching the horror movie *Texas Chainsaw Massacre* when they decided to get married.

'It was just crazy, man,' Alexander told *Access Hollywood*. 'And we were just looking at each other and said, "Let's do something wild, crazy. Let's go get married, just for the hell of it."' It was 3.30 a.m., and this being Vegas the couple did not need to wait long to tie the knot. Britney was wearing ripped blue jeans, a skimpy black top and a baseball cap as she and Alexander hopped into the hotel's limousine and asked the driver to get them to church so they could wed.

The first two chapels the driver took them to were closed, but then they pulled up at A Little White Wedding Chapel, which married Vegas couples around the clock. They handed over the $70 fee for a marriage licence and signed their names on the dotted line. Then it was time for the impromptu service, which featured a live piano player and a bouquet of pink roses.

The bellman walked Britney down the aisle to the strains of the wedding classic 'Here Comes the Bride' and the ceremony, which lasted just seven minutes, ended at 5 a.m. Onlookers said the couple were 'smiling and laughing' throughout. Charlotte Richards, the wedding chapel's owner and one of its ministers, told *Today* that the two were sober. 'We do not marry anybody who is inebriated,' she insisted. 'They have to be fully aware of what they are doing.'

They then returned to the hotel and spoke with Spears' friends. She told them how happy she was, but, said Alexander, none of them offered any form of congratulations. So, the couple drank some celebratory champagne and thought about where they could go on honeymoon. Eventually, they fell asleep. It had been a long and eventful night.

When Britney woke up some hours later, she was 'a little stunned' that she had tied the knot, according to a friend who spoke to her several hours afterwards. As news spread of what had happened, plenty of other people were stunned too – more than a little. Lynne spoke to her daughter on the phone and left her in no doubt that she disapproved.

At first, wrote Lynne, she assumed her daughter was telling her a 'distinctly unfunny joke'. When she realized it was no joke, she was 'fuming'. She remembered Alexander as a child, when her sister had said, 'It would be the worst curse in the world if one of our girls grew up to marry this one.'

Britney's brother Bryan spoke to Alexander and told him that the marriage was absolutely going to be annulled. This was an important step because an annulment dissolves a marriage as if it never happened, while a divorce recognizes that it did occur, which can bring financial and other issues into play. It was this that was on her manager's mind when he allegedly sent Britney a curt message: 'Congratulations, you just gave away half your money.'

Alexander's family were also taken aback by the news as it reached them. His father, Dennis, was busy at work under the bonnet of a truck when a journalist approached him for comment. 'What y'all talking about? My boy's not even in Vegas!' The story itself was surreal enough, but it became even more so when some started to claim that the Jason Alexander who had married Britney Spears was the dumpy, balding actor of the same name from US comedy *Seinfeld*.

Soon, Britney's management team and family were descending on Vegas to try to get the mess cleared up as swiftly as possible. Alexander said that some 'mean-looking suits' and 'power men from LA' put pressure on him to walk away. He agreed to annul the marriage, and it was formally closed at 12.24 p.m. on 5 January. 'Plaintiff Spears lacked understanding of her actions to the extent that she was incapable of agreeing to the marriage,' the annulment petition had stated.

It took the judge about two hours to act on the 'complaint

for annulment' filed at 10.12 a.m. in Clark County Family Court. Judge Lisa M. Brown signed the uncontested order. 'There is no marriage now,' said Spears' attorney, David Chesnoff of Las Vegas. 'Jason agreed to this completely. They've made a wise decision. I know they care about each other. They are friends.'

The petition had laid out the terms for the annulment. It stated: 'Before entering into the marriage the plaintiff and defendant did not know each other's likes and dislikes, each other's desires to have or not have children, and each other's desires as to state of residency. Upon learning of each other's desires, they are so incompatible that there was a want of understanding of each other's actions in entering into this marriage.'

Alexander said he was driven to the airport and handed a ticket for a flight home. Rumours that he was paid half a million dollars to annul the marriage have been disputed. He claimed that when he had signed the annulment papers, Britney had been unable to meet his eye.

For Alexander, the aftermath of his brief marriage to one of the planet's most famous celebrities has been mixed. Naturally, he initially got a lot of attention. He hired an agent and appeared on reality television programmes and chat shows and bought a new car, but he soon ran out of money. In 2022, he was arrested for stalking, and he will make a dramatic cameo in the final chapter of this book.

Although it was theorized that Britney's abrupt decision to marry was as a reaction to news that Justin Timberlake had got engaged to Cameron Diaz, most people now think the marriage was simply a joke that went a bit far. On her website, Britney ran a message from her attorney, stating, 'They are simply two young people who regret what they have done.'

During an interview with *People* magazine, she said, 'That thing was a total ugh ... I was not in love at all.' Later, she was able to laugh it off, telling fans at a live show: 'You may be lucky; I could end up marrying you!'

However, this impulsive and reckless episode in her life would have less fun implications. In retrospect, it was another step on her journey towards the conservatorship, as it painted a picture for her parents of a young woman wildly out of control and in danger of putting herself in compromising situations at the flick of a finger.

In her memoir, Jamie Lynn writes that her big sister was behaving in a 'paranoid and erratic' manner after the Vegas episode. One day, she writes, Britney told her: 'Baby, I'm scared' and grabbed a large knife from the kitchen. She then pulled Jamie Lynn to her room and locked them both inside. Britney placed the large knife in the bedside drawer and said again: 'I'm scared.' Jamie Lynn added that 'everyone was too invested' and 'didn't want to do what should have been done' to help Britney at this stage. Britney has denied the presence of a knife, tweeting to her sister: 'I've never been around you ever with a knife or would I ever think to do such.'

Within months, Britney was engaged again, and within months of that she was on marriage number two. She and Kevin Federline had met when she was still with Timberlake.

She was impressed with him, later describing him to *Details* as 'not a shallow mother-f**ker, Hollywood actor guy'. His school yearbook had declared him 'most likely to be seen on *America's Most Wanted*'.

He was dating a former model and actress called Shar Jackson when Britney and he bumped into each other in Los Angeles. Federline and Jackson's budding family included their first child, a girl called Kori, and two children from a former relationship of Jackson's. A fourth child was on the way, so when Federline phoned from LA to tell Shar that he had been 'hanging out' with Britney, she was livid. She told him he was 'a dirty dog'.

Later, Shar acknowledged that the headlines the episode sparked were not unhelpful to her. 'In a sick, twisted way the Britney thing has put my name back out there. I'm now working with my group trying to finish our album,' she told Female First. As for Britney, she spoke of Federline's dumping of Shar in sacrificial, romantic terms. 'He did it for me,' she said.

Britney announced her relationship with Federline to the world by contacting paparazzi photographers and summoning them to the Beverly Hills Hotel, according to *Britney: Inside the Dream*. There, the snappers found her emerging with her new man. They drove in her white Mercedes to Santa Monica with the photographers in tow. At the beach, Britney, wearing cropped denim shorts and a white summer shirt, leapt with joy onto Federline's back and he carried her to the water's edge.

As the photographers continued to snap away, the couple

strolled along the beach and then sat on the sand. Britney removed her shirt to reveal a yellow bikini top, and more photographs were taken. Eventually, Britney told the pack: 'You got your pictures ... can y'all go away now.'

She had cleverly masterminded the entire episode. The media had photographs aplenty, she had sent out the message that she was over Justin Timberlake, and she had given Federline a quick crash course in what life with her was going to be like. Britney was to suffer terribly in the glare of the media's lenses in the future, but on this day, she had been in charge.

Their relationship announced to the world, Federline joined Britney for the European leg of her world tour. They had matching tattoos depicting lucky dice inked onto the inside of their wrists. The next stage seemed almost inevitable. 'All of a sudden I said, "What if you want to get married?" And I kind of went from there to asking him if he would marry me,' she told *Entertainment Weekly*.

Initially, Federline said 'No,' because he felt it was more traditional for the man to propose. A few minutes after turning her down, he proposed and she accepted. For her engagement ring she chose a 5-carat diamond with a double platinum band and used her own money to buy it because Federline couldn't afford it. This was remarked upon in the media, some quarters of which accused Federline of being a 'gold digger'.

By becoming engaged to the Princess of Pop, Federline had reached a new height of media celebrity himself. Soon after he popped the question, they were photographed walking on the beach at Marina del Rey. Britney was in an impish mood, wearing a T-shirt with the slogan: 'I'm a virgin ... but this is an old T-shirt'.

They were married on 18 September in a non-denominational ceremony at their wedding planner's residence in Studio City, California, filing legal papers on 6 October. Britney wore a white strapless gown designed by Monique Lhuillier. Lynne thought she looked 'like an angel'. Originally, more than 300 invitations had been sent out for a big ceremony in Santa Barbara. However, after the media had got wind of the plan, the couple scaled it down to a smaller bash, with only twenty-seven of their closest friends and family invited.

Nevertheless, Britney was thrilled when she saw that hundreds of hot-pink and red roses had been called in, to make it the sweetest of ceremonies. The invitations for the event had stated that it was just an engagement bash, rather than a full-on wedding, so it was a surprise when guests arrived and discovered that this was a wedding ceremony, with outfits waiting upstairs for those who were not dressed in suitable garb.

Jamie gave Britney away, and her cousin Laura Lynne gave a speech as chief bridesmaid. When Laura Lynne handed Britney the wedding ring, the bride accidentally dropped it. The female minister assured her that this was a harbinger of good luck. Federline told Britney he was 'so proud to be your husband'.

After the ceremony, Britney changed into a more revealing white mini-dress and then the revellers moved onto the Xes

(From left to right) T. J. Fantini, Tate Lynche, Ryan Gosling, Nikki DeLoach, Britney Spears, Christina Aguilera and Justin Timberlake. The Mickey Mouse Club was a star-making factory.

LEFT: Before the turbulence began, a your Britney with her family *(from left to right)* Jamie Spears, grandfather June, Bryan, Jamie Lynn, Britne and Lynne.

Baby,
one more time
isn't enough.

9 out of 10 girls don't
get enough calcium. It takes
about 4 glasses of milk
every day. So when I finish
this glass, fill it up, baby.
Three more times.

got m

MIDDLE: The perfect face for advertising.

LEFT: Kicking off the ... Baby One More Time tour in style.

ABOVE: Celeb royalty. Britney and Justin were untouchable at the top until it all fell dramatically apart.

LEFT: Britney and Lynne Spears at the 1999 Teen Choice Awards.

LEFT: Flying high. Britney poses with four trophies at the 1999 MTV Europe Awards, winning best female singer, best pop act, best song and best breakthrough act.

MIDDLE: Britney made a star appearance on *Sabrina the Teenage Witch*, teaching Sabrina a dance and telling her that sometimes being surrounded by people 'is the loneliest place to be'.

RIGHT: By 2002, Britney was starring in her own film, the widely panned *Crossroads*.

LEFT: One of the most famous MTV Video Music Awards performances in history.

BELOW: Another iconic performance, Britney and Madonna stunned the world with a steamy on-stage kiss as they opened the 2003 VMAs.

LEFT: Carefully choreographed photos with new boyfriend Kevin Federline.

RIGHT: When Britney's life fell apart, it fell apart quickly. Numerous admittances to rehab and an ongoing custody battle led to a now infamous forty-eight hours.

Weather: Cloudy and cold, 34/19   SPORTS ★ FINAL   Friday, February 23,

DAILY NEWS

50¢   NEW YORK'S HOMETOWN NEWSPAPER   nydailynews

MORE EXCLUSIVE PHOTOS INSIDE

BRITNEY'S FURY!

Troubled star goes wild outside the home of her estranged husband, Kevin Federline.   PAGES

BERNIE WILLIAMS' YANKEE HEARTACHE SEE

LEFT: Few fans watching Britney's Circus tour in 2009 knew that the star's every move was now managed under the constraints of a conservatorship.

MIDDLE: The *X Factor* threw Britney into a new, more intimate limelight, but she struggled with anxiety as her fans got so close.

LEFT: With on-off manager Larry Rudolph.

ABOVE: Performing the show of a lifetime at her Las Vegas residency. As Britney continued her wild career, many began to question the conservatorship.

MIDDLE: #FreeBritney! Confetti fills the air as the pop star regains control of her life.

RIGHT: A happy fresh start with husband Sam Asghari.

nightclub in Los Angeles. By this stage, Britney was wearing a pink sweatsuit, complete with the logo 'Mrs Federline', while his was emblazoned with the legend 'The Pimp'. Their first dance was to 'Lights' by Journey. Revellers ate ribs and chicken.

The wedding was not officially finalized on the day, because a delay had meant that prenuptial arrangements had not been agreed. Legally, this might have meant that Federline could have claimed half of Britney's fortune. The legal papers they signed stated, 'Britney understands and agrees that the alleged wedding ceremony in which the parties intend to participate shall not be a lawful Californian marriage.' The couple would exchange legally binding vows a fortnight later.

Not everyone thought the marriage was necessarily a good idea. The couple had only been back in touch for a matter of months when they wed, so although it was not as recklessly entered into as the Alexander union, it still felt impulsive to some. Lynne disapproved of the fact Federline already had a child and had asked her daughter to take things slowly. She didn't give the couple her blessing.

The couple honeymooned in Kentwood and Fiji. Naturally, this trip was of huge interest to the media. Britney was angry when she and her new husband were on the cover of *Us Weekly* under the headline 'Britney's Private Album!' Other pictures of the couple's honeymoon, including images of them eating breakfast on the beach, were plastered across five pages inside the magazine. Although Britney was used to the intrusive eye of the media, she felt that the press had crossed a line here. Fuming, she consulted with her team to draw up a response.

'Kevin and I chose a resort location where we were promised absolute privacy and seclusion,' she said in a statement. 'Unfortunately, staff members took photographs of us, which we allowed them to take once we were assured they were being taken only for private use in a scrapbook they gave us as a souvenir.' There was a feeling of naïvety here. Indeed, *Us Weekly* was in no mood to be contrite. In a counter-statement, the magazine said: 'Coming from a celebrity who sold pictures of both her wedding and her stepdaughter, it's unlikely the issue here is privacy.'

They continued, 'Could it be that Britney is seeing red after not seeing the green from these photos? Britney Spears should start a magazine if she'd like to dictate her own coverage.'

The media focus on their marriage was intense. For Britney, this was a more familiar experience than it was for Federline. When newspapers obsessively speculated on how long their marriage would last, it was an alienating experience for him. Then an ex-girlfriend of his appeared in the press, claiming he didn't brush his teeth or wash properly. Nevertheless, the couple were initially very happy, by all accounts. Britney was 'more balanced' and 'doing well', writes Jamie Lynn, and any 'emotional fluctuations' were 'well managed'.

The couple lived at the Fairmont Miramar Hotel in Santa Monica while they waited for their new home to be ready, choosing to stay in one of the resort's bungalows, which set them back $1,000 per night. Privacy was the priority, and no expense would be spared to keep them away from the invasive lenses of the media.

Privacy was also a major factor in their choice of a $7.5 million mansion. The Mediterranean-style contemporary property included a two-storey complex and 1.4 acres of wooded hillside. There were six bedrooms and seven bathrooms. It was set in a gated community, to allow them some much-needed seclusion. Other celebrities, including the actor Mel Gibson, lived nearby. When Jamie visited, he was agog and kept saying that it felt more like a holiday resort than a home. His daughter had come a long way.

She tried to pass on some of her success to her new husband, who had aspirations to become a rapper. He released two singles, and later an album called *Playing with Fire*. Britney had endured a couple of negative reviews in her time, but nothing could prepare her, or indeed Kevin, for the reception his album received.

'A lot of the songs ... are not good even judged by the standard of "he did it just to make you mad" because they're too weak to even inspire any ire,' said *Rolling Stone*. *Now* magazine, meanwhile, said, 'His flow is generic and instantly forgettable and his lyrics are trite, inconsequential and full of self-importance.' *Vibe* felt that 'his constipated, region-nonspecific flow overwhelms even the most flamboyant beats', and *Slant* said, 'This disc is just as disposable and dumb as you'd expect.'

The album sold just 6,000 copies in its first week, debuting at number 151 on the *Billboard* 200. Despite the album's poor critical and commercial performance, Federline's music opened up a path for him that meant he was away from home a lot. Britney was unimpressed by this, as she was in no mood to have a third man absent from her life, after Justin and Jamie.

With one man signing into her life, Britney dispatched another. After nine years and five albums together, she and Larry Rudolph parted ways – though it wasn't to be the last time she would work with him in what would become an on–off relationship. 'Britney and I simply realized that we have done all that we can do,' he said in a statement at the time. This changing of the guards was imitated in her art, when she covered the Bobby Brown song 'My Prerogative' in 2004, also naming her first greatest hits album after the tune.

When the couple announced that they were expecting a baby, there were hopes things would become more stable. Britney gave birth to their first son, Sean Preston, almost exactly a year after they wed. On 14 September 2005, she underwent a C-section at the UCLA Medical Center in Santa Monica.

News she had given birth to a boy shocked many, because the media had been strongly predicting that her baby would be a girl. Mother, father and child stayed in a private suite on the facility's fifth floor, with minders standing guard and searching any visitors the couple permitted through the door. They settled on the name for the boy after Britney had suggested they call him Charlie, while Kevin opted for Kevin Junior.

A nurse told the media that 'like all new moms, Britney

was very nervous' and was 'constantly asking if the baby was okay'. Another said that Britney 'couldn't get any peace of mind', and her anxiety over her baby son was such that she couldn't get to sleep. After Britney returned home, her anxiety continued; she wouldn't believe that the scar from the C-section would ever fade.

Then it was time for the baby shower celebration. Dozens of snappers descended on the neighbourhood in the hope of grabbing a precious photograph of Sean Preston. In the melee, a photographer was shot in the leg with a pellet gun. Brad Diaz, one of the paparazzi stationed at the foot of the Malibu home's driveway, was clipped in the thigh by the plastic bullet, according to the *Los Angeles Times*. 'It could've been somebody driving by, walking by,' said a local cop. 'We have no idea where it came from.' The incident has never been explained.

Even as she tussled with the challenges of pregnancy and motherhood, Britney was still a loving sister. Jamie Lynn was then playing the lead in kids comedy drama series *Zoey 101*. When Britney learned that one member of the cast was making fun of her sister behind her back and spreading false rumours, she turned up on set – heavily pregnant – to have some stern words with her. 'Are you making fun of my sister?' she asked of the co-star. 'Telling lies and spreading rumours? You shouldn't do that!' She added that she would not keep being offered acting jobs if she got a reputation as a bully. The actress, who was later dropped from the franchise, later claimed she had been bullied on set.

Motherhood is a shock to most first-time mums, and

Britney was no different. In the early months of 2006, a number of incidents drew criticism from the press. She was snapped with Sean Preston on her lap as she drove, and two months later he fell from his highchair and had to be taken to hospital. Then a photographer took photos of Sean Preston's baby seat facing the wrong way in Britney's car.

The couple insisted that she had been forced into these erratic behaviours because she was constantly swamped by photographers. 'If she feels like she gotta take the baby and put him on her lap and get out of there, so be it,' Federline told GQ. As for Britney, she said, 'I made a mistake and so it is what it is, I guess.'

The media found it easy to criticize Britney, but they were less harsh on themselves after another incident. She had stopped at the Malibu Country Mart and unbuckled her baby from the car. Photographers immediately surrounded mother and child like a pack of hungry jackals, with no mercy or compassion at all. No sooner had she turned away from the snappers than she realized that the staff in a nearby restaurant were also taking photos of her on their mobile phones. The mid-noughties were a curious time for celebrities like Britney. She was more than used to being caught by press photographers, but the advent of camera phones meant she now faced a second wave of intrusion from everyday people who wanted to grab their own pictures of her. From only feeling safe when there were no paparazzi around, celebrities could now never feel they were free from an intrusive 'click'.

Britney sat down at a table in the restaurant and burst into tears holding Sean Preston. From time to time she would look up, tears rolling down her devastated, traumatized face, and see that the photographers were still there and they were still clicking away. The images would earn the snappers a tidy sum, and here was documentary proof that they had little mercy when it came to their prey. Even as a mother sobbed with her baby son, rather than back away, they snapped ever more hungrily, mindful that the sadder she looked, the more lucrative the images would be.

Support or sympathy for Britney was in short supply among these photographers. A rare example was when a member of the paparazzi was moved to quit his job with a photography agency in protest at the 'aggressive' pursuit of her. Nick Stern, a British worker for the Splash news agency, said that high-speed convoys of photographers' cars and motorbikes tailing the star were a danger to her and the public. 'Directly or indirectly, Britney is going to come to some horrific end, or a member of the public will,' he predicted.

It had felt for a long time that the pressure of the paparazzi would eventually lead to someone being harmed. Jamie Lynn has written of when she and a friend were taken to the local pet store by Lynne and Britney. As they left the shop, a mob of photographers and onlookers surrounded the store and the family's car. Eventually, the family got into the vehicle, but as Lynne tentatively tried to take it forward through the mob, a man screamed that she had run over his foot. He told his wife to call the police. Luckily, a medic was able to establish that the man was entirely unharmed, but the scary memory haunted Jamie Lynn for years.

Partly in a bid to throw a scrap of material to the media

in the hope their pursuit would become less intense, Britney appeared in the 2005 reality television series *Britney & Kevin: Chaotic*, which consisted of their home videos. The series also saw her open up about her life. The five-episode series aired in May and June 2005 and chronicled the couple's relationship from their meeting to their engagement and wedding. To say it went down badly would be an understatement. Taylor Carik of *Flak Magazine* considered the series an 'insult to common sense and decency', and Josh Wolk of *Entertainment Weekly* felt that it was 'career suicide by videocam', because 'the truth is not only that she's vapid, but that she's self-obsessed to a dangerous degree'. Aaron Beierle of DVD Talk described it as 'an absolutely unwatchable and horrifying trainwreck of a series'.

Later, Britney would join in with the kicking the series received, remarking that it was 'probably the worst thing I've done in my career'.

Britney's second son, Jayden James Federline, was born on 12 September 2006, just forty-eight hours before his older brother's first birthday. Kevin drove Britney to the UCLA hospital in Santa Monica, where she had her second caesarean birth. Just two months later, Britney stunned Kevin when she filed for divorce.

However, when it came time to take the plunge, she seems to have had second thoughts. 'Do you really want to do this?' she asked him as the two met to discuss final details of their divorce. When he confirmed that he did, Britney replied, 'You're the biggest mistake I've ever made, but thank you for my babies.'

Then the two took a cigarette break before finalizing the terms of their split. A 2004 prenup agreement dictated that Federline would get $250,000 for each year of their marriage, but, according to reports, Britney was so keen to get the negotiations finished that she increased that figure to $500,000. Speaking to MTV, she tried to explain more why the marriage did not work out. 'I think I married for the wrong reasons,' she said. 'Instead of following my heart and doing something that made me really happy, I just did it for the idea of everything.'

When she filed for divorce she requested sole custody of the couple's children, with Federline only granted visitation rights. Just twenty-four hours later, he made a counter-request, asking for sole custody for himself. In the days after this, she was photographed in a leopard-print mini-dress so short it revealed her underwear, and then photographed again, getting out of a car in a hiked-up mini-skirt. Celebrity blogger Perez Hilton accused her of deliberately engineering the photographs for attention and publicity. He has always taken a cynical view of celebrities, but within months it would be clear that all was not well with Britney.

To have had two children so close together was challenging for Britney. It would be challenging for any woman but all the more so for one in the public eye. Jamie Lynn remembered that her 'fun-loving and sweet-natured' sister 'lost her softness'. She became distant again, 'even when we were sitting 3 feet away from each other'. Britney became 'moody', and her 'erratic behaviours' were 'troubling' the family. In time, she became 'agitated' and 'angry enough with Momma to yell at her in public'.

She also began to concern the public. When she stumbled and nearly dropped baby Preston, the watching world gasped in judgement. Few paused to consider that the only reason they saw that stumble was because Britney was surrounded by photographers and cameramen, bringing chaos to the star's life.

Speaking to *Access Hollywood*, Britney said it had been 'kind of bad with the paparazzi'. As for Lynne, she stood by her daughter as she faced a tidal wave of criticism and judgement, asking, 'How has America become so self-righteous?'

Nevertheless, Lynne could tell that Britney was not in a good place. She admits, though, that she had no idea of the scale of the problem. Lots of testing events were coming Britney's way. When Lynne's sister Sandra died at the age of fifty-nine, this only added to the pain that was building inside Britney. With her marriage over and the challenge of bringing up two children adding to the pressure that was forever on her young shoulders due to her fame, Britney began to wobble.

Chapter Seven

BALD AND BROKEN

Her most shocking moment to date came in February 2007, when Britney casually walked into Esther's Haircutting Studio in San Fernando Valley, California. It is a small, modest salon, but it was about to become the centre of one of modern showbiz's most infamous moments. Earlier, Britney had turned up at Federline's house and demanded to see their sons, but he allegedly refused, prompting a downward spiral that became clear to everyone when Britney arrived at the salon.

She reportedly told the owner that her hair extensions were too tight and that she wanted all her hair shaved off. Esther Tognozzi refused, but this was not about to stop Britney. She grabbed a pair of hair clippers and shaved off her hair – all of it. Outside, photographers looked on with excitement as they snapped every moment of this meltdown. Onlookers, who quickly joined them at the window, were aghast.

Britney reportedly told another customer that she was shaving her hair because she wanted people to stop touching her and was tired of having 'things plugged into her'. However, the newly skin-headed Britney quickly regretted her move. She started to cry and said, 'Oh my god, I shaved it all off. My mom is going to be so upset.'

Not that these tears were enough to stop her moving from the salon to a tattoo parlour. Britney reportedly asked for a tattoo of another woman's lips to begin with, then a small cross. The tattooist later told the media that she felt an 'insane sense of anxiety and energy that felt so negative'. She asked Britney why she had shaved her hair and the singer replied, 'I just don't want anybody, anybody touching my head. I don't want anyone touching my hair. I'm sick of people touching my hair.'

She then returned to her home in Malibu, where her team convinced her to see a doctor. Donning a black wig to cover her cropped cranium, she arrived at the Cedars-Sinai Medical Center in Beverly Hills. Meanwhile, Lynne was on her way to LA from Louisiana, having received another SOS call regarding her daughter's wellbeing. She wrote later that she was 'devastated' and 'broken'. She said she prayed to God to 'protect' her daughter. Jamie also tried to get through to Britney, giving her a talk over dinner. Later, she was spotted singing karaoke in the Roxy bar on Sunset Strip. Wearing a blonde wig and sunglasses, she seemed to be enjoying herself until someone put '... Baby One More Time' on.

Just a day before the shaving incident, Britney had stayed for less than twenty-four hours at an offshore drug rehabilitation facility in Antigua. Now, Lynne, Jamie and members of Britney's team tried to convince her to give rehab a go, but this time at a different centre: Promises in Malibu. Britney was unreceptive to the idea initially. She complained that her mother was trying to 'force' her into taking the step. She eventually agreed to go there for four weeks but ultimately only lasted a day.

The initial development was announced via a statement from her team. 'Britney Spears has voluntarily checked herself into an undisclosed rehab facility today,' it said. 'We ask that the media respect her privacy as well as that of her family and friends at this time.' Nevertheless, the world continued to look on, agog, at what was happening to this young celebrity. There was much speculation over what had prompted her meltdown and why she had chosen to express it via her hair.

A psychotherapist said that a woman shaving her head bald was an attempt to de-sexualize herself. A psychoanalyst, Bethany Marshall, told ABC News that Britney was 'acting out' with the gesture. 'The hair represents the stylists, the handlers, people who are in control of her life and manage her looks,' Marshall said. 'Now she's saying, I'm in charge of my looks.' Dr Alistair Roff, a social psychologist, told *The Times*: 'This is not so much a cry for help as a cry of "leave me alone!"' The media absolutely went to town on the story. For reporters, it was irresistible: a top-tier celebrity in a very public and symbolic breakdown. Fox News said this was 'shear madness' and ABC News said Britney was 'bald and broken'.

As for Britney, she has spoken since about the episode. During her MTV documentary *Britney: For the Record*, she said it was prompted by her split with Federline. 'He had just left me and I was devastated,' she said, adding that the shaving of her hair was a 'little bit of rebellion, feeling free, shedding stuff'. She said there was 'so much artificial stuff' going on, adding, 'People thought I was, like, going crazy … but people shave their heads all the time.'

In a footnote typical of celebrity culture in the digital age, strands of hair Britney left on the salon floor were quickly posted on eBay. There are reports the bidding reached $1 million before the auction was removed from the site because the hair could not be authenticated. The hair later resurfaced for sale on a new website: buybritneyhair.com, where it was offered alongside the clippers Britney used, the Red Bull can she drank from and a blue lighter she left behind.

Britney's stay in Promises lasted just a day. She checked out in the early hours of 21 February and returned home to Malibu. She felt the home was empty and incomplete without her children there, explaining later that 'my babies represented home'. She couldn't sleep properly or settle back in. She checked into the Bel-Air Hotel, but still she found it hard to relax and switch off from the demons that were haunting her mind. Following a meeting with her legal team about the situation with Federline, she drove to his house to ask if she could see her sons. He refused to open the door, and this prompted another public drama for her.

She left the house as the passenger in a Mercedes. When the car stopped for gas at a Mobil station in Tarzana, paparazzi swarmed around the car, flashbulbs firing and Britney feeling ever more violated in the front seat. They continued to chase her car down the road before suddenly the car's brake lights went on as it ground to a halt. What happened next put Britney back on the front pages.

She sprang out of the car, brandishing a green umbrella. She strode to the SUV belonging to one of the photographers and attacked it with the umbrella. The photographs of her during the attack showed Britney livid. 'F**k off, you motherf**ker,' she screamed. 'Stop following me, leave me be. I just want to see my kids.'

In the documentary *Framing Britney Spears*, Daniel 'Dano' Ramos, who photographed Britney attacking his car with the umbrella, did not emerge from the interview sympathetically. 'She never gave a clue or information to us that, I don't appreciate you guys, leave me the eff alone,' Ramos claimed, to which the director asked, 'What about when she said, "Leave me alone"?'

Regardless, Britney later apologized for the incident. 'I apologize to the pap for a stunt that was done four months ago regarding an umbrella,' she wrote on her website. 'I was preparing my character for a role in a movie where the husband never plays his part so they switch places accidentally. I take all my roles very seriously and got a little carried away. Unfortunately I didn't get the part.'

Around this time, she also spent a night sleeping in a parking lot, according to court papers filed subsequently. The day after the umbrella incident, Britney returned to Promises. Her family and management tried to wrap a supportive arm around the star. Her father said, 'We've got a sick little girl here – we're just trying to take care of her.'

She went back into rehab in Malibu and stayed for some weeks this time. When she left, her on–off manager Larry Rudolph put out a statement saying that she had been 'released' after 'successfully completing' her programme. Jamie was conciliatory towards Rudolph, saying that when the manager convinced Britney to go to rehab, 'he was doing what her mother, father and a team of professionals with over 100 years of experience knew needed to be done'. He added that his daughter had been 'out of control' and that Rudolph had been chosen 'to roll up his sleeves and deliver the message to save her life'.

However, from Britney's point of view her family was ganging up against her. She felt that they were leveraging her desperation to see her sons against her to force her into rehab. She struggled to know who to trust and ultimately turned against her family and management. She stopped talking with her mother, who she felt had sided with Federline against her.

In June, Britney was spotted delivering a stiff note to her mother, in which she said she wanted to be left alone. After she had delivered the letter, she told reporters that she was 'praying for' her mother, in what was interpreted by some as a deliberate pop at her mother's religious image.

As her life unravelled, Britney was charged with a hit-and-run offence and driving without a valid licence. The charges, which each carried a maximum penalty of six months in jail and a $1,000 fine, came when she was accused of hitting a parked car and driving away. Two months later, a judge dismissed the case after an out-of-court settlement was reached with the person whose car she struck.

The case was off her shoulders and she was able to see her children again, but the negative publicity over recent events would not be so easily sorted. Britney realized she had to reach out to her fans who had been perplexed by her recent dramas. She penned a heartfelt letter on her website. Its message: 'I was so lost.'

'Recently, I was sent to a very humbling place called rehab,' she wrote.

> I truly hit rock bottom. Till this day I don't think that it was alcohol or depression. I was like a bad kid running around with ADD.

> I was so overwhelmed I think that I was in a little shock too. I didn't know who to go to. I realized how much energy and love I had put into my past relationship when it was gone because I genuinely did not know what to do with myself, and it made me so sad.

She also wrote of how she had been too open and naïve in her dealings with the world. 'Being in that vulnerable state and taken to dinners and parties with friends and finding out later you paid for everything was a huge learning lesson for me,' she explained. 'I think the whole problem was letting too many people into my life. You never know another person's intentions or what another person wants. I feel I was too open and looking for answers when I had it all to begin with. I have had to cut so many people out of my life.'

She added that she felt she was being unfairly regarded because she is a woman. 'It is like when you are a real woman and say what you feel and how you think things are supposed to be,' she wrote, 'that people just say you are a "bitch".' Putting her children at the heart of the message, she concluded: 'I am sitting here and it is 6.25 and both of my sons are asleep. I am truly blessed to have them in my life.' It was distress over being separated from her boys that was at the heart of her recent crisis, Britney felt. Being back with them felt so good.

Her message hit home for many, and she began to receive a fair amount of understanding. Lynne, for instance, later wrote that when Britney attacked that SUV, 'she was acting out my fantasy'. For Lynne, the relentless criticism of her daughter in the media was hard to watch. In 2001, she remembered, Britney started crying when one of the newspapers commented that she had put on a couple of pounds in weight. 'It was so mean-spirited, overblown and hurtful,' Lynne wrote.

While all this was going on, throughout 2006 and 2007 Britney had recorded her next album. During promo interviews for *In the Zone*, she told *Entertainment Weekly* that she was already writing material for her next project. Henrik Jonback, who co-wrote with her for the album, said they wrote songs in the bus and in her hotel room between concerts. During their relatively short time together, he noted how wild Britney's life was. 'I got a good look into the hysterical life of a superstar, and I must say, I'm very happy not to be one myself,' he reflected afterwards.

She originally wanted the album to be called 'The Original Doll' and spoke about using it as a symbol of her taking control of her affairs. In a statement on her website, she wrote,

> I think I should rephrase myself from my previous letters when I was talking about taking a 'break'. What I meant was I am taking a break from being told what to do … It's cool when you look at someone and don't know whether they are at work or play since it's all the same to them. The things I've been doing for work lately have been so much fun, because it's not like work to me anymore. I've been even more 'hands on' in my management and the business side of things, and I feel more in control than ever.

Part of that control, she told *People* in a separate conversation, was wanting to explore the sounds of her childhood in Louisiana. 'When I was little, I would listen to myself … But the record label signs you, and you're just thankful to get a hit song. You can't really show off your voice and where you came from. I would like to try to have more influences of that sound. Not that I'm going to be like frickin' Tina Turner. But you never know,' she said.

Working with her was J. R. Rotem. 'It's definitely Britney, but the next level,' he said. 'With songs like "Toxic", she was very innovative, and we're trying to top it. Push it to the next thing.' She also got praise from songwriter Keri Hilson. 'She was so focused,' Keri told *OK!* of the sessions. 'She gave 150 per cent. She had already been recording throughout her pregnancy. We started in Vegas and continued in LA and worked at her house. When we worked at her house … it was only three weeks after [Jayden] was born. I mean, focused? I don't know any other mother that would do that.' Producer Kara DioGuardi told *Extra* that Britney 'worked really hard' and called her 'unstoppable'.

'It's Britney, bitch' begins the opener to new album *Blackout*. 'Gimme More' is a strong track, but it lacks the clout of '… Baby One More Time'. Co-written by Jim Beanz, Marcella 'Ms Lago' Araica, Nate 'Danja' Hills and Keri Hilson, it veers between pop, dance pop, electropop and EDM and proves to be musical hypnosis itself.

The sighing and moaning vocals of 'Piece of Me' would have made lots of listeners want just what the title suggests. MTV said it is 'as if she's offering herself up on a platter' before she presents herself as bad karma and asks the listener again – are they sure they want a piece of her? As one reviewer remarked, 'Was this a promise or a threat?' Another said that although this is a song 'about life under the lens', it's 'hardly a paparazzi whinge: Britney's delivery is a mix of sneer, threat, come-on and shrug'.

On 'Radar', the electro sound is boosted by sonar pulses and distorted synths, but the effect was described as one-dimensional by some. 'Break the Ice' is better. As one of the writers, Keri Hilson, remarked, 'It's about two people, a girl and a guy, and the girl is saying, "You're a little cold. Let me warm things up and break the ice."'

That multi-layered electro R&B is followed by 'Heaven on Earth'. 'It is a very honest song,' said writer Nicole Morier.

'Get Naked (I Got a Plan)' comes next. The duet between Spears and Danja sees them sing about sex with their voices distorted: his sounds like a decaying moan. 'Freakshow' is a dubstep-flavoured track about being in the spotlight, while in 'Toy Soldier' she channels her Destiny's Child best as she sings about needing a new man. Another notable track is 'Ooh Ooh Baby', complete with flamenco guitar and a similar melody to her future track 'Womanizer'.

The reviews were not often kind. 'What's pop's most plastic princess to do when her life has turned into absolute gold for the tabloid masses?' asked *NME*. 'Turn into a robot!' Mike Schiller of PopMatters was also less than thrilled. 'Right down to its utterly garish cover, *Blackout* is utterly disposable and ultimately forgettable,' he wrote. Andy Battaglia of the A. V. Club said *Blackout* 'counts both as a significant event and as a disquieting aberration that couldn't be more mysteriously manufactured or bizarrely ill-timed'.

Still, Margeaux Watson of *Entertainment Weekly* said, 'There is something delightfully escapist about *Blackout*, a perfectly serviceable dance album abundant in the kind of bouncy electro elements that buttressed her hottest hits.'

'Spears's fifth studio album is her most consistent, a seamlessly entertaining collection of bright, brash electropop,' wrote Dennis Lim for *Blender*, adding that he enjoyed her 'mix of righteous resentment and self-mocking humor'. Alexis Petridis of the *Guardian* listened to the album through a filter of Britney's recent woes. 'These days, when you hear Britney Spears singing about going insane or feeling her brain spin like a hurricane, what you picture is not a woman delirious in the midst of coital ecstasy,' he wrote, 'but those photos of her, freshly scalped, attacking a paparazzo's car with an umbrella and looking as disturbed as it's possible for a human being to look without actually being strapped into a straitjacket.' He gave the 'bold, exciting album' four stars out of five.

'Robert Frost said the world will end in one of those two ways, consumed by passion or frozen by rationalism, and it's clear which option Brit will take,' said Melissa Maerz of *Rolling Stone*. 'But meanwhile, she's gonna crank the best pop booty jams until a social worker cuts off her supply of hits.'

Kelefa Sanneh of *The New York Times* had been harsh on *In the Zone* but was more positive about *Blackout*. 'Unlike all the other Britney Spears albums, this one hasn't been accompanied by the usual avalanche of magazine interviews, talk show appearances and televised performances,' he wrote, but 'that doesn't make it any harder to delight in how good the best songs sound'.

For the first time, a Britney album did not debut at the top of the charts in the US, instead coming in at number two, with first-week sales of 290,000 copies. By the end of the year, it had shifted a very respectable 3.1 million copies worldwide. The declining sales should be understood through the prism of a dramatic reduction in album sales across the board, as the music industry wrestled with the march of technology. However, there was a growing sense that Britney was going through a very rough patch in her life.

At the 2007 VMAs, Britney put in a very disturbing performance. According to reports, she had been out partying in Las Vegas into the early hours the night before, and she certainly presented herself on stage as someone who had done just that.

Britney seemed dazed and uninterested, putting in what felt more like a casual soundcheck than a rehearsal proper. As she mimed, often unconvincingly, to 'Gimme More', there was little life to her performance. At times it seemed she might topple over. Then, she covered her face, seemingly uncomfortable with the light. The broadcast occasionally cut to celebrities in the audience, such as Rihanna and 50 Cent, who seemed aghast and amused by the spectacle in front of them.

Britney's outfit was a black sequined, studded bikini with fishnet stockings. When she got backstage after the slot, she burst into tears and said she looked fat. Then came the verdicts. 'Britney Spears phoned it in for her "comeback" performance,' said the *Daily News*. The *New York Post* said it was 'totally lame, pathetically lip-synched' and that Britney was 'visibly nervous [as] she tottered around the stage, dancing tentatively and doing nothing that sounded or looked like real live singing'. Britney, who had previously dominated coverage of the awards show when she performed with a snake, became the dominant story here for all the wrong reasons.

On the TV show *The View*, Barbara Walters said, 'The lip-synching didn't work,' while Whoopi Goldberg felt Britney was 'like a bad stripper'. Pop blogger Perez Hilton said the performance was 'so bad it was embarrassing'. The fact it had been her first broadcast performance for three years and she was on edge wasn't considered.

'She was just plain nervous because of all the hype and she's embarrassed,' a source told *People*. Several people, including Simon Cowell, predicted that the performance was so bad it would end Britney's career. Cowell's verdict was ironic given how their paths would cross in the future. However, *Vogue* has since said it was 'undeniably iconic' and praised her for providing the only memorable performance of the night.

One voice for her defence became an iconic moment in her story and in the narrative of fan videos on the internet. A nineteen-year-old called Chris Crocker uploaded a video onto YouTube, in which they reflected on what Britney was facing at the time. They talked about the deaths in her family, a divorce, a custody battle – and tearfully, hysterically pleaded with the world to 'Leave Britney alone!'

The video quickly went viral, and Crocker's hysteria was widely mocked. Their statement that they would 'jump off the nearest f**king building' if anything happened to Britney was just one of the passages that was ridiculed. However, speaking to NPR years later, Crocker said that the message of the video was strong and serious, regardless of what people thought of the delivery.

'I always felt that if people just read the transcript and

didn't pay attention to how I looked or that I was screaming and just read what I said, there's nothing comical about it,' they said. 'Like I was listing the fact that Britney had lost her aunt. She was going through a divorce. She just had kids and, you know, I was scared she had post-partum [depression] or something. Like there was nothing funny about anything I was saying.'

At this stage, a rather inscrutable character called Sam Lutfi entered the story. There have always been conflicting accounts of who he is and how he came to take such a controlling position in Britney's life. But certainly for her mum and dad, he was a key player in the process that led to Britney being placed under a guardianship. According to the account in Lynne's book, he originally contacted her anonymously and told her that drugs had been planted in Britney's house as part of a conspiracy between Britney's team and Federline.

Lynne remembered that she arranged for the house to be searched, but no drugs were found. Some months later, she received a second call from the same man, she wrote. He insisted that there were drugs in Britney's house; they just hadn't been found yet. However, he added, he was calling with a business proposition: he wanted Lynne to sell jewellery products on a television shopping channel. Lynne agreed to meet him and found he was a 'man in his late twenties or early thirties who appeared to be of Middle

Eastern heritage'. She added that he was wearing a 'ratty' baseball hat, a T-shirt and jeans and was 'sweating profusely'.

An air of mystery surrounded Lutfi. According to public records, he was born on 16 August 1974 in Los Angeles. Music magazine *Blender* reported that he grew up in Woodland Hills, where his mother reportedly owned a number of fuel stations. He has sometimes been described as a film producer, and the film website IMDb states that he served as associate producer on the 1998 film *Circles* (also known as *Crossing Paths*) and 2001's *Crossing Cords*.

His story is not without controversy. According to the *Los Angeles Times*, in 2005 businesswoman Jumana Issa filed a complaint against him, claiming he had harassed her after he demanded that she cancel a payment that had already gone through. The claim was dismissed in 2006 because Issa failed to appear for a preliminary hearing.

Court documents show that Issa accused Lutfi of sending her obscene emails, offensive faxes and late-night voicemails, as well as hanging up on her around fifteen to twenty times a day. Issa described the ordeal as 'an overwhelming nightmare'.

The *Los Angeles Times* also reported that, in October 2004, a restraining order was issued demanding Lutfi stay at least 100 yards away from Mark Douglas Snoland, a neighbour in Lutfi's condominium building, for three years. The petition for a restraining order claimed that Lutfi began 'pounding' on Snoland's front door one night in September 2004. Snoland also claimed other instances of harassment by Lutfi, including repeated phone calls followed by hang-ups.

In his response to the petition, Lutfi claimed he only 'knocked' on his neighbour's door and that Snoland 'was never threatened' but was simply angry at being removed from the board of the condo complex.

The accounts of how Lutfi came to meet Britney herself are as contradictory as they are vague, but Lynne was unimpressed by Lutfi and the hold she felt he had on her daughter after they were introduced. She claimed there was a situation of tight control and manipulation, with Lutfi 'calling the shots on her medications, cutting her phone lines, and deciding who's let in to see the pop star', said the *Los Angeles Times*.

Lynne was even less impressed when he took, as she saw it, complete control of her daughter's life: 'He appointed himself as her gatekeeper, and there was no one he wanted to keep the gate closed to more than Britney's family,' she said in her memoir. The *Los Angeles Times* offered its own, damning assessment, describing him as a 'shady hanger-on who controlled everything – from doling out her pills to holding the paparazzi's leash'. However, ABC News reported Lutfi's insistence that he actually reunited Britney and her mother after a lengthy estrangement. In court in 2012, he produced a photograph he had taken of Lynne and Britney smiling in front of the singer's Malibu home. 'I spent months working on a reconciliation, and this is the day of the reunion,' he said.

Jamie Lynn offers a similarly negative assessment of Lutfi. She writes that he 'weasled his way into her life with big stories and empty promises'. She remembered telling her mother that she found him 'creepy', writing, 'To me he seemed both pathological and manipulative.' She accused him of tipping off the paparazzi and then lying about it, making appointments with producers and isolating her sister from their parents.

She recalls an occasion when Britney felt 'uncomfortable' because a producer had turned up at her home without her knowledge or agreement. She ran upstairs and locked herself in a bedroom, begging Jamie Lynn to get rid of the producer for her. In the wake of this incident, she became 'increasingly more erratic'. Lutfi denies any wrongdoing, but Britney has since taken out a number of restraining orders against him.

At the start of 2008, Britney's frustration over her distance from her children again erupted into a full-blown crisis. On 3 January, she endured legal meetings where she was asked pointed questions about her parental abilities. The questions did not sit well with her, and she eventually became convinced that Federline was planning to block her from ever seeing her children again. That evening, when Federline's bodyguard Lonnie arrived to collect the boys, who were at Britney's home for a visit supervised by a monitor, she declined to co-operate or hand them over.

The monitor who was supervising the visit managed to get Sean Preston out of the house and into the bodyguard's car, but when they returned to the house for Jayden, Britney had locked them both in the bathroom. Almost immediately, this escalated into a major drama. Television news channels described it as a 'hostage' situation and ran footage of ambulances, police and fire crews descending on Britney's home. The whirr of TV helicopters was heard as they hovered above the property. As the evening wore on and the sky darkened, they trained their spotlights onto Britney's home.

At the time, Lynne was in Connecticut with Jamie Lynn, who had recently announced that she was pregnant. When Lynne learned about the situation with Britney and the boys, she felt 'frantic' and 'sick', she later wrote. She felt torn between the needs of her pregnant sixteen-year-old daughter and her twenty-six-year-old daughter who was clearly in the middle of a major crisis. When she saw footage on television of the scene at her elder daughter's home, she was 'horrified'.

Eventually, Jayden was freed, although there are disputed reports over how this was achieved. As for Britney, she was strapped to an ambulance trolley and taken out of the house. The images of her dazed face were beamed around the world. Lynne said the sight of her daughter's 'beautiful brown eyes, pained and haunted' absolutely broke her.

Britney was driven to Cedars-Sinai Hospital. It was a dramatic journey, with sirens blazing and a police escort. On arrival, she was placed under an involuntary 5150 psychiatric hold. This refers to a section of California's Welfare and Institutions Code which can be enacted if a person is a danger to themselves or others, or if they are 'gravely disabled'. For most individuals this is a serious development. However, when that person is worth millions and millions of dollars, the stakes are that much higher. Under this hold, Britney was supposed to stay in hospital for three days, but she discharged herself after twenty-four hours.

With dozens of photographers surrounding her home, Britney did not want to return there, so she and her new boyfriend, Adnan Ghalib, drove to Mexico. They checked into a modest, $110-a-night hotel in the city of Rosarito. Britney wore a pink wig and a pair of spectacles and faked a cockney accent. They were photographed purchasing a pregnancy test kit. That test proved to be a false alarm.

Soon, they returned to Los Angeles and to reality. While Britney had been in hospital, a judge had suspended all her visitation rights and given sole custody of the boys to Federline. At the end of January, these simmering tensions boiled over when Britney had a row with Sam Lutfi after a prolonged period of sleeplessness. The police took her to the UCLA hospital. Again, there was melodrama, when a dozen motorbikes, two cars and a helicopter were deployed to take a single stunned woman to hospital.

When the officers arrived, Lynne asked them what their grounds were for taking her daughter. They barked at her that they had their orders. As they strapped Britney down, Lynne asked if this was necessary and was told in no uncertain terms that she, too, would be arrested if she caused any problems. Then Britney started to call out for Lynne, crying, 'Mama! Mama!' Lynne asked if she could ride with her daughter, but the police refused. She was driven to the hospital and again sectioned under a 5150 order, her second in a month. Britney's life was about to change dramatically.

The following day, James Spears was given control of his daughter's affairs and financial assets under a temporary conservatorship. The die was being cast for Britney's future.

Jamie went to the LA Superior Court, where, in a closed hearing, Judge Reva Goetz granted a temporary conservatorship. The judge also granted a restraining order against Lutfi. Lynne wrote that 'tears of relief and joy' filled her eyes. 'Thank you. Thank you. Thank you, God,' she thought. 'I could be Britney's mother again, and Jamie could be her daddy.' Britney could not have known at this stage that the arrangement would become permanent and change her life.

So it was that Britney's life ground to a standstill, when she had her rights curtailed under a court-sanctioned conservatorship that put decisions about her life and fortune – and even her body – in the hands of others, most significantly her father. Attorney Andrew Wallet was also made a co-conservator of the estate.

The ruling meant that Jamie had the power to bar people from visiting his daughter in hospital, that he could take sole control over her medical records and that he could cancel any contracts she may have signed. Unusually, he had been named conservator of Spears herself after Goetz told a packed courtroom that conservatorship over her person was necessary and appropriate, saying, 'It is in the best interests of the conservatee to have conservatorship over her person.'

According to the terms of the arrangement, Britney was blocked from making key decisions, personal or financial, without approval. As *The New York Times* reported, even 'her most mundane purchases, from a drink at Starbucks to a song on iTunes, are tracked in court documents as part of the plan to safeguard the great fortune she has earned but does not ultimately control'.

The arrangement also came with an enormous symbolic power. Under US law, conservatorship is the appointment by a country of a guardian or protector to manage the financial affairs and/or daily life of another person, due to old age or physical or mental limitation. As the old age and physical categories did not apply to Britney, here was a clear sign that her parents did not believe she was mentally capable and that an independent judge agreed with that assessment. For Britney, her life and image would never be the same again.

A friend of the family, Jacqueline Butcher, said that days after the arrangement was put in place in 2008, she heard an interesting and revealing exchange between Jamie and Britney. Speaking to the *New Yorker*, she explained what she heard: 'Jamie said, "Baby…" and I thought he was going to say, "We love you, but you need help." But what he said was, "You're fat. Daddy's gonna get you on a diet and a trainer, and you're gonna get back in shape."' Butcher also made another eye-opening claim, saying that if anyone questioned a decision Jamie had made on behalf of his daughter, he would counter: 'I am Britney Spears!'

Meanwhile, the real Britney Spears had another hearing at the same court house to deal with, as her life became more about dates in court than dates in concert arenas. At one custody update, MSNBC correspondent Janet Shamlian described the scene as a 'zoo' and 'embarrassing'. Her TV crew was one of a hundred outside the court, alongside photographers from around the world. The mood was frantic and Shamlian wondered aloud why so much attention was being devoted to this hearing when there was a presidential election afoot.

When Britney arrived, the scene descended from that of a zoo into something even more feral. As she stepped out from her car, she was surrounded by a media mob and said, 'I wanna get back in the car ... let me get back in the car!' Federline arrived in a more orderly manner, and it was no surprise to anyone when his emergency sole custody was extended and Britney lost visitation rights. When Britney left one hearing, she sparked a meme when she yelled, 'Eat it! Lick it! Snort it! F**k it!' before bursting into tears.

After Britney was released from the hospital, her parents released a statement reading, 'We are deeply concerned about our daughter's safety and vulnerability and we believe her life is presently at risk. There are conservatorship orders in place created to protect our daughter that are being blatantly disregarded. We ask only that the court's orders be enforced so that a tragedy may be averted.' There were several extensions, but the conservatorship was set to expire at the end of the year.

Things got worse for Britney in several ways in the fall. In September, Lynne published her memoir *Through the Storm*, including details of events in the run-up to Britney's 'breakdown'. The memoir proved so upsetting for Britney that Jamie Lynn made the decision not to read the book at all. 'I saw first-hand the difficulties that Momma and Britney suffered after my sister read it, and I wanted to avoid the possible outrage reading her words would evoke,' wrote the younger sister.

The following month, the temporary conservatorship was made permanent, giving Jamie control of the singer's personal and financial affairs indefinitely. Judge Reva Goetz said, 'The conservatorship is necessary and appropriate for the complexity of financial and business entities and her being susceptible to undue influence.' In the legal papers supporting the bid, Britney was described as an 'adult child in the throes of a mental-health crisis'.

Probate judges in California are allowed to appoint two kinds of conservators: ones responsible for a person's physical and mental health, and others who are put in charge of an individual's finances. In Britney's case, both happened. Later, Adam Streisand, a Los Angeles-based lawyer hired by Britney after her hospitalization in 2008, gave an insight into her state of mind at the time, including how aware she was of what was happening around her. He told the *New York Post* that even when she was near rock-bottom, Britney did not appear crazy but 'just agitated'. He added, 'She has expressed to me very strongly that her father not be the conservator ... There has been an estrangement for quite some time. With him as conservator, that is causing her more agitation and more distress.'

However, claimed *Today*, it was a development the singer 'apparently' approved of, because a court-appointed attorney said the details had been explained to the twenty-six-year-old and she agreed not to oppose. Still, Britney was far from overjoyed. 'I think it's too in control,' she said during an interview with MTV. 'If I wasn't under the restraints I'm under, I'd feel so liberated. When I tell them the way I feel, it's like they hear but they're really not listening … It's like, it's bad. I'm sad.' She continued, 'There's no excitement, there's no passion.' And then: 'Even when you go to jail, you know there's the time when you're going to get out. But in this situation, it's never-ending.'

After Goetz blocked Britney from having Streisand represent her, she hired attorney Jon Eardley to appeal the decision. Eardley immediately claimed that the conservatorship was granted without the necessary five days' notice and was therefore invalid. However, in something of a catch-22, under the rules of the conservatorship Britney was unable to appoint her own legal personnel without the involvement of her father or his lawyer. Weeks later, an MTV documentary called *Britney: For the Record* was released, offering what would become a rare glimpse into her life. 'I've been through a lot in the last two or three years,' she told the interviewer, adding, 'I'm sad.'

This was a rare statement by Britney about the situation at this stage, but she still had her music to express herself. It was time for her to return to the music and release her sixth album, the aptly named *Circus*. She said from the start that she wanted to lighten things up a bit after what she described as the 'dark and edgier and urban' themes of *Blackout*. 'It is a little bit lighter than *Blackout*,' she said on her website. 'I think a lot of the songs I did at that time, I was going through a really dark phase in my life, so a lot of the songs reflect that.'

She recorded it in the US and Europe at a number of studios including Legacy and Sony in New York, the

Underlab in Los Angeles, Frou Frou Central in London and Bloodshy & Avant Maratone in Stockholm. 'The process was cool, because I got to write a lot of the songs, and in the beginning, I really took part in that,' she said. 'I experimented with a lot of the pop producers that I worked with on my earliest albums. I went all the way back old-school, which is a lot of fun to do.'

Although the album's title was clearly an allusion to what a circus her life had become, Britney said it was also less metaphorical than that. 'I like the fact that you're always on the edge of your seat when you're at a circus ... You're never bored,' she said. 'You're just really engulfed in what's going on around you. And you want to know what's going to happen next.' Metaphorically and literally, the album title certainly felt well timed.

It begins with the sirens and the catchy, repetitive chorus of 'Womanizer', a track described by Britney as a 'girl anthem'. 'Circus', the second song, was an electronic dance song that saw Britney sing about her life 'in the centre of the ring'. Here, we felt the effect of her conservatorship for the first time. Previous tracks, dating as far back as 'Stronger', hinted at how her life would develop, but this was the first expression of them during the conservatorship itself. 'Kill the Lights' also covered life under the spotlight, specifically her relationship with the paparazzi.

Later, in the *New York Times* documentary *Framing Britney Spears*, a former *Us Weekly* employee admitted to spending around $140,000 per week on paparazzi photos. Britney's song is an expression of these sorts of gobsmacking transactions. 'Is that money in your pocket/Or you happy to see me?' she sings. It is easy to hear it as a companion track to 'Piece of Me'.

Comparatively, in 'Shattered Glass' it is a cheating lover she is addressing. She asks him if the girl he cheated on her with was worth it and promises to haunt his dreams. He has broken everything they had, like shattered glass, and now, she vows, his own life will fall apart the same way.

'If U Seek Amy' managed the unlikely achievement of seeing Britney compared with Irish author James Joyce. When spoken aloud, the song's title sounds like 'F-U-C-K me'. *Slate* magazine asked, 'Has Britney pioneered a new kind of dirty pun?' It ran through past examples of steamy wordplay in culture, starting with blues pianist Memphis Slim, who recorded a wistful 'If You See Kay' about his lost girlfriend in 1961. In 1977, lo-fi pioneer R. Stevie Moore released a track with the same title, as did Canadian band April Wine in 1982 and pop-punk band Poster Children in 1991. Meanwhile, in 2005 Norwegian punk band Turbonegro went one letter longer when they put out 'If You See Kaye'.

When Irish band The Script performed the same feat, they acknowledged a debt to James Joyce – noting that he used the 'If you see kay' gag in *Ulysses*. However, the legendary Irish author also managed an even ruder trick in the same passage, when he wrote, 'See you in tea.' Before leaving this theme, it is worth noting that in 1991 rockers Van Halen also released an album called *For Unlawful Carnal Knowledge*.

NME said 'If U Seek Amy' was one of the filthiest songs of all time, while AllMusic said the song is 'a Katy Perrystyled exercise in crass commercial carnality that is at once the best and worst song here'. Some took the track as a reference to Amy Winehouse, with its lyrics about 'smoking up' and drinking. It was released as the 'Back to Black' singer was becoming notorious for her addiction issues. Whether Amy is a reference to Winehouse or an alter ego for Britney herself, this is one of the most defiant songs on the album.

Another electropop belter, 'Unusual You' deals with a woman finding unexpected love and has been noted as a 'pulsating ballad', also drawing comparisons to the 'shimmering waterfall mood first popularized by Janet Jackson'. She sings that she was once 'someone else' and felt almost as if she were a boxer, forever being forced to defend herself to her critics. None of them knew what she's really like behind the scenes, she sang. 'Blur', which sees Britney exploring the lower register of her vocal range, is more urban, dealing with the morning after a party.

'Mmm Papi' saw a resurrection of the criticism Britney faced for '… Baby One More Time'. The lyrics were dismissed by some as having Lolita themes, but many listeners would be too taken by the Latin pop tune to worry too much about that. More potent for some ears is when she sings that there are 'too many people' around her. Was this another passing allusion to how crowded and penned in she felt by her conservatorship?

Her vocal performance on 'Mannequin' drew criticism from some reviewers, but in truth the track should have attracted for its futuristic and experimental production. The trip-hop flavour is perfectly rendered. 'Lace and Leather' is the sort of funk that drew comparisons with everyone from Janet Jackson to Prince to Vanity 6.

'My Baby' was written by Britney about her two sons. The song seemed to divide everyone. A reviewer for the *Orange County Register* complained that 'Brit's grating faux-Janet Jackson vocal, its inadvertently funny greeting-card lyrics and life-without-you-is-nothing phoniness' left them 'feeling insulted'. The *Los Angeles Times* said it was 'a reminder that Spears is still a young woman trying to manage an impossible situation'.

The bonus track, 'Radar', had originally been destined for *Blackout* but was usurped for that album by 'Break the Ice'. Here, she is on more familiar pop ground: the lyrics refer to an attraction between the protagonist and a man, with the woman unclear if he knows what she is feeling. The vocals, though described as 'threatening' by one reviewer, bring to mind Rihanna, and it takes a cold-hearted listener not to be at least slightly keen to bounce along with it.

'There are decent tunes here, and hooks that sink into you with ruthless efficiency, not least the chorus of "Womanizer", but you expect cutting-edge pop to deliver not just hooks and tunes but a degree of sonic daring,' said Alexis Petridis of the *Guardian*. '*Circus* isn't bad as pop albums go, but whether by default or design, it's substantially less edgy and exciting than its predecessor,' he continues, concluding that 'the sound of Britney back on track is substantially less interesting than the sound of Britney going off the rails'. He gave the album three out of five stars.

The *Los Angeles Times* gave her just two out of five for *Circus*. 'The lyrics about Britney as mannequin, sex object, paparazzi victim and leather-clad mistress have grown tedious,' said Ann Powers. 'When the wittiest one is based around an adolescent text-message-style joke, you know it's time to refocus.' On America's other coast, Jon Pareles of *The New York Times* said he enjoyed the 'crisp' songs and 'catchy melodic interludes'.

The *Independent* was rather harsher. Its reviewer looked back at *Blackout*, describing it as a 'grisly, charmless car-crash experience', and said that *Circus* was 'almost as charmless [but] at least it succeeds better than its predecessor in their intention of portraying the former Mouseketeer as some kind of robotic nymphomaniac doll'.

In a return to form for Britney in the US, *Circus* debuted at number one on the *Billboard* 200, her fifth of six albums to reach the top of the chart. The album spent nine weeks in the top ten, making it Spears' longest-running top-ten album since *Oops! ... I Did It Again*, which spent twenty-three weeks in the top ten in 2000. It enjoyed platinum sales in the UK and the US and reached global sales of 4 million. It also became only her second studio album after her debut to spawn two top-ten singles and three top twenty singles. It was also her first to have two top-five singles in the United States, along with five charting songs on the *Billboard* Hot 100.

Those healthy figures were boosted considerably by the concert tour she embarked upon to promote the album. The Circus Starring Britney Spears was her seventh concert tour. She would open the shows with a hard-hitting trio of 'Circus', 'Piece of Me' and 'Radar'. She would close the sixteen-track set strongly, too, with 'Toxic', '... Baby One More Time' and 'Womanizer'.

Stacey Plaisance of the Associated Press wrote that the tour was a 'tightly choreographed, if perfunctory performance'. Ann Powers of the *Los Angeles Times* stated that 'Spears can safely call this performance a success'. However, *People* writer Chuck Arnold felt that she 'never really hit her old stride'.

Another promotional date for the album came when Britney appeared on the UK reality show the *X Factor*. She had stopped in London for over a week earlier in the year, and Simon Cowell hoped she would swing by the *X Factor* studio. He had wanted her on the show for some time, even though he had mixed feelings about her. He admired her as an artist who had 'taken charge' of her career, seeing her as a 'game changer [who was] prepared to die while trying'. However, he had not always been so complimentary: following the MTV Music Awards he dismissed her as a 'plain Jane'.

According to Tom Bower's biography *Sweet Revenge: The Intimate Life of Simon Cowell*, when he finally booked her for the show he was taken aback at her antics and demands. Bower recounts how Britney's team insisted there would be 'no rehearsal' amid 'chaos' following her arrival at the studio. She had demanded two luxury trailers when most stars were only assigned one, and then changed her mind and took Cowell's old dressing room instead. According to Piers Morgan in *The Sun*, large placards were quickly erected on the walls, adorned with slogans including, 'You are an AMAZING dancer', 'Everybody LOVES you' and 'You're going to NAIL IT tonight'.

The producers were then told that Britney was on medication and that they must ensure the studio was 'in lockdown'. Britney ignored the show's finalists and initially refused to meet Cowell. 'She's frosty and I haven't got a clue why and I don't care,' he said. He was eventually granted access to her room, where she informed him she had never watched the show. In a humorous bid to break the ice, Cowell told her: 'Touch me, I'm human.'

On stage, she mimed her song 'Womanizer' because, according to *Sweet Revenge*, she 'forgets her lines'. However, other reports have suggested that she mimed because she wanted to focus on her dance routine rather than her vocals. There was also criticism of Britney for not supporting the show's contestants backstage, as other celebrity guests had done in the past.

Indeed, when presenter Dermot O'Leary asked her on-air what she thought of the acts, she dodged the question, saying, 'Yes, awesome, thank you. Amazing, I met so many different people, the place is beautiful.' This landed badly with audiences, who were still under the impression that both the judges of the show, and the celebrities who popped in week by week, were taking a keen, coach-like interest in the hopefuls.

The *Daily Mail* said 'she lip-synched badly, danced unconvincingly and appeared stunned when asked about the relative merits of the contestants', all of which suggested 'all is not quite as it seems'. Piers Morgan wrote that, 'based on this diabolical performance and her pathetic antics behind the scenes, from a professional point of view Britney is finished'.

However, in 2008 media coverage of Britney began to touch on the restraints she was living under. In an early alarm bell over the guardianship she was under, the *Daily Mail* suggested that sources said, 'In private she confesses to feeling pressurized to perform, frequently dissolves in tears and has a volatile love–hate relationship with her father.' The paper reported that Britney was not allowed to drive her car or choose her own meals. 'She cannot leave her father's side without permission – and then only with chaperones,' it said. 'All her phone calls are monitored and she is watched over day and night by guards.'

Tensions were said to be high behind the scenes, as Jamie booked her in for engagements ranging from the one-off appearance on the *X Factor* to a worldwide tour. A tearful Britney is said to have threatened to cancel some appearances, complaining that she was not yet strong enough to cope. 'She blames her father for everything,' one acquaintance told the *Daily Mail*. 'He and Brit hardly spoke for years and now all of a sudden he is the king.

'She has an overwhelming love–hate relationship with her dad, and now Jamie has alienated his daughter by treating her like an infant. She is given to crying fits and says her father has pushed her into performing before she is ready.' The guardianship was so draconian that *Rolling*

Stone writer Jenny Eliscu, who interviewed Britney a few months later, wrote, 'She has about as many legal rights as when she was in the Mickey Mouse Club as a little girl.'

After the *X Factor* appearance, Britney dropped out of an associated engagement. Thousands of fans had squeezed into London's Astoria club to see her, only to leave disappointed after they were informed she was 'too shy' to go on stage. There were shades of the frustration London fans had felt when she let them down at the premiere of *Crossroads*.

However, the core fact for the UK trip was how her appearance boosted the *X Factor*'s ratings to 12.8 million – a record high. Backstage after the show, Cowell had given up trying to get a conversation out of the star and walked off. For him, the figures mattered much more than the level of friendliness. It would not be the last time the two would be together on one of his shows.

Britney looked like a young woman who needed some stability in her life, but even as she thought she had found it, it arrived clouded by the legal restrictions she found herself under. She began a relationship with Jason Trawick, her agent from the prestigious William Morris Endeavor. Ten years older than Britney, he was hoped to be the sort of stable, mature figure who could bring some order to her existence. In April 2012, he was officially made a co-conservator. Suddenly, he could control Britney's decisions on everything from food to clothing to medical care – but not her assets. If this feels a strange turn of events, then that's because it is. 'This is a very unusual situation, because generally you don't see conservatees get married,' attorney Jeffrey S. Cohen, who wasn't involved with the case, told *People*.

The guardianship was going to get more unusual before it came to an end. Britney was under a lens. The longer the conservatorship wore on, the more her wider life began to be viewed through it. For instance, when company Brand Sense Partners sued Britney in 2011, it led to question marks that had wider ramifications, including over the appropriateness of the conservatorship.

During the dispute over a licensing agreement for one of her fragrances, lawyer Geoffrey A. Neri argued that the singer had to be capable of testifying. He argued in court papers that she takes care of her children, makes numerous public appearances and was then on a seventy-nine-date tour across much of the world. 'The notion that Britney Spears is mentally or emotionally unfit to testify under oath is a sham,' Neri wrote.

Although in that case and two others Judge Goetz ruled the singer mentally too fragile to testify, the question mark raised by Neri threw into doubt whether the conservatorship arrangement was appropriate. There was a similar contradiction later, when, after years of maintaining that the singer was too vulnerable to be questioned, her conservators agreed to a deposition by Britney in a lawsuit filed against her and her father by Lutfi. Britney, who was wearing a magenta blazer and pearls, testified without any issues, a public refutation of the guardianship. Some wondered whether her parents' assessment of her mental state varied depending on which answer was most useful to them.

Soon after, she was back to posting on Instagram, including an image captioned, 'All energy is contagious.' Hundreds of supportive comments flooded in from fans seemingly well aware of the latest legal twist in her life. 'You have gone through hell and back again but you have persevered every time,' one wrote. 'You got this.'

What the fans wanted was for Britney to return to what she did best – and they were in luck. Britney has always had a knack of finding a jaw-dropping track to open an album, and she managed it again with her next release. *Femme Fatale* was a longer time coming than most Britney albums: she worked on it from the summer of 2009 until 2011 was on the brink of springtime. 'Till the World Ends' opens with sirens, though they are not as wild as those at the start of 'Womanizer'. Written and produced by pop royalty Kesha, Dr Luke, Alexander Kronlund and Max Martin, it oozes gravitas and makes everyone listening sit up and pay attention. This might have been Britney's seventh album, but she was not resting on her laurels at all.

This up-tempo dance- and electropop song was, from the moment it was completed, destined to liven up parties around the world. It is a pure hands-in-the-air party anthem. Britney's life away from the spotlight may have been tumultuous, but this was a comeback tune to thrill her fans.

Any fears that the album could only slump downhill after such an iconic opener were assuaged by 'Hold It Against

Me'. A song that had previously been earmarked for Katy Perry, it fell into Britney's lap, and the industrial beats of her team's production made it perfect for her.

Still, the song created a short-term legal headache for Britney just when she didn't need one. The Bellamy Brothers slammed it for being a bit too similar to their 1979 hit 'If I Said You Had a Beautiful Body Would You Hold It Against Me'. In a statement, David Bellamy said, 'Professionally, well, in all honesty, we feel completely ripped off. Where's the originality?' However, for those letting themselves go in clubs as this banger blasted out of the speakers, this was not an issue. Britney's producer Dr Luke filed and then dropped a defamation lawsuit against the brothers after they withdrew their allegation that he had copied their work.

'Inside Out' features more electropop with mind-blowing synths. 'I Wanna Go' is about losing your inhibitions and features Britney apologizing for her sexual needs. It was written and produced by Max Martin and Shellback, with additional input from Texan songwriter Savan Kotecha. Britney has often spoken fondly of the song and the team behind it: 'There is nobody I feel more comfortable collaborating with in the studio,' she said of Martin. The infectious, pre-chorus whistle they added into the production is memorable. *Washington Square News* said that although 'it is not an innovative song', it is 'fantastically effective and endlessly enticing with its liberating, toss-your-cares-away, dance-like-a-complete-and-utter-fool cathartic chorus, repeated words and typically saucy Britney lyrics'.

'How I Roll' is playful and bubbly, with an almost

playground-chant feeling to the chorus. '(Drop Dead) Beautiful' is also a bit of fun. Together, the two songs are a welcome change of pace from the nightclub bangers that open the album. 'Seal It with a Kiss' felt like a filler for many, an album track that was merely making up the numbers. However, the chorus is surely punchy enough to justify its inclusion.

On the house track 'Big Fat Bass', she collaborates with will.i.am, who wrote it as a celebration of the bass sound and its enduring influence on the club music scene, but it also has a double-meaning allusion to ... something else. Speaking to *Rolling Stone*, Britney said that she is a fan of the Black Eyed Peas because the band 'make incredibly catchy, fun pop/dance records and I LOVE will.i.am's style – I have always wanted to do a song with him and would love to work with him more in the future. He is so interesting.' The song definitely had a flavour of the Black Eyed Peas to it. will.i.am returned the compliment to Britney, writing on his blog, 'Thank you Britney for collaborating it was a pleasure working with you. Thank you for trusting my instincts. You're a doll.'

'Trouble for Me' drew comparisons to Janet Jackson, while 'Trip to Your Heart' once more performed that very Britney trait of taking lyrics that look on paper as if they are part of a pop ballad and setting them to a bigger, clubby track. 'Gasoline' is one of the more forgettable tracks of her career and felt incomplete to some reviewers.

From the moment Britney first heard 'Criminal', she felt it was quite different to anything she had ever performed before. With its folky flute melody, it truly is new ground for her. Although the song concerns her love for a dangerous guy, this is one of the least aggressive tracks on the album.

Unlike almost everything on *Femme Fatale*, it could almost have sat on her debut album. When she brought it out as a single, she felt it needed serious treatment for the video. 'So I really wanted to deliver this song,' she told MTV. 'I was thinking of a really cool concept for the video just to make it interesting.' The deluxe edition also included 'Up n' Down', 'He About to Lose Me', 'Selfish' and 'Don't Keep Me Waiting'.

Kitty Empire of the *Observer* said that 'a more accurate title' for the album 'might be "In Season" [because] these are twelve all-out mating calls, issued on an endlessly pulsating dancefloor, in which Spears dispenses with any other subject matter save her unquenchable lust'. She said the 'standard is high' on the album and 'it would be tempting at this point to say that Britney is on fire' but sufficed to say, 'She's hot to trot.'

Alexis Petridis of the *Guardian* said that though he didn't want to sound like he was 'wishing the woman ill', there's 'no doubt Britney Spears made her best album when she was at her worst', because on *Blackout* she 'finally appeared to reveal something of her personality'. On *Femme Fatale*, he complained, her voice is 'as anonymous as ever, a state of affairs amplified by the lavishing of autotune', and he accused her of doing 'what pop stars invariably do in lieu of having a detectable character of their own: go on and on about sex'. At its best, it 'sounds like a party, with a cutting-edge pop soundtrack', he wrote, but 'the question of precisely what Britney Spears brings to said party remains as imponderable as ever'. He gave the album three out of five stars. Rich Juzwiak of the *Village Voice* also dismissed her vocals, writing that her 'voice doesn't add much to the conversation'.

The *Independent* was harsher still. 'Perhaps chastened by the disasters that seemed to result whenever Britney's private life became her public image, all traces of authentic character, issues, attitude and emotion have been ruthlessly excised from *Femme Fatale*, leaving the hollowest possible shell of corporate entertainment fodder,' wrote Andy Gill. He compared Britney unfavourably with a new kid on the block: 'As far as novelty goes, her natural demographic now has an icon as quirky and characterful as Lady Gaga to fascinate and fuss over, a performer who doesn't expect simply to keep milking the same cash cow without at least a costume-change,' he wrote.

Slant magazine remarked, 'The success of a Britney song rests almost entirely on the quality of other people's songwriting and production, and almost every track on *Femme Fatale* succeeds or fails on that basis.' A track that *Spin* felt succeeded was the 'disco banger "Till the World Ends"', which it adjudged as her 'first truly synapse-sizzling single since "Toxic"'. However, PopMatters felt that *Femme Fatale* was 'just a big dumb club album'.

Thank goodness, then, for *NME*, which wondered whether this might be 'Britney's best ever record'. It was 'always going to be a wild card', wrote Ailbhe Malone, 'and luckily, it is, but in the good way'. *Femme Fatale* 'brims with the laidback confidence of someone who knows she's back on top'. Jody Rosen of *Rolling Stone*, too, felt that it 'may be Britney's best album; certainly it's her strangest'.

Tom Gockelen-Kozlowski for the *Daily Telegraph* wrote that despite 'her weak voice and empty lyrics', Britney had 'placed herself at the avant-garde of pop with this masterful mixture of über-cool dubstep and sugary pop [that] exceeds the eccentricity of Lady Gaga without putting a phone-shaped hat anywhere near her head'.

Femme Fatale debuted at the top of the charts in Australia, Brazil, Canada, Mexico, Russia, South Korea and the United States. This left her in a four-way tie for third most number-one albums for a female artist, along with pop royalty Mariah Carey, Janet Jackson and Beyoncé. It reached the top ten in twenty-four countries, enjoyed platinum status in the US and the UK and became the first of her albums to have three top-ten singles in the US charts: 'Hold It Against Me', 'Till the World Ends' and 'I Wanna Go'.

Although the conservatorship was already restricting Britney's life, her career was continuing apace. She was ready to take a new path that would bring her into the living rooms of millions, but, as ever, it would not be an easy ride.

Chapter Eight

THE *X FACTOR*

By 2013, it was time for Britney's career to take a path that she would find more challenging than expected. Given how chaotic, and for Simon Cowell infuriating, Britney's performance on the UK *X Factor* had been, some might have been surprised when she was chosen by Cowell as a judge for the second season of the US version of the show. However, the ambitious reality television boss has always looked at the bigger picture rather than letting personal feelings get in the way of making his shows a hit.

His tie with Britney began when Julia Carta, a makeup artist known to Cowell, was booked for Britney's world tour in 2011. As they travelled round the world, Carta would ask Britney about her future plans. Britney said she wanted a new challenge and Carta mentioned the *X Factor* as a possibility. Having launched her own career through appearances in talent shows, Britney was receptive to the idea. 'It would be great to give others a start in that way,' she said, adding that she thought Cowell was 'a class act'.

'There was a time where I think everybody was trying to up themselves in terms of who could find the biggest known star to be on a panel,' Cowell told the *Ellen DeGeneres Show*, citing *American Idol* judge Jennifer Lopez and 'the other one … blondie' in a disparaging reference to Christina Aguilera on *The Voice*. 'And so we thought, "Well, we'll take Britney."'

A conference call was arranged, and Britney was so excited by the idea that she lost her sass for a moment and weakened her bargaining position. 'I'm in,' she said. Her on–off manager Larry Rudolph, who was back in favour at this stage and also on the call, said, 'We don't have a deal yet!' But Britney was not in the mood to play it cool. 'No, I'm in,' she said.

Hiring Britney was a major coup for Cowell but also a significant gamble. During series one of the US show, he had dropped a clanger when he hired former Girls Aloud singer Cheryl Cole as a judge. She was dropped within weeks of the series starting after she failed to connect with US audiences. Nobody knew who she was and nobody cared to make the effort to find out. Her north-east England accent also proved problematic for US ears. Pussycat Dolls singer Nicole Scherzinger was moved from co-hosting duties to replace Cole on the judging panel. Her co-host, former T4 presenter Steve Jones, continued as a solo host, but he also failed to connect with US audiences and contestants alike, so Cowell was under immense pressure to make the Britney appointment work.

When word spread that Cowell has signed Britney, there was plenty of comment, much of it negative. Before she had judged a single contestant, she was being written off. Some people inevitably filtered the news through her rivalry with Christina Aguilera, who had appeared as a judge on rival show *The Voice*. It was suggested she had signed up to try to overshadow her rival. However, the cash was a major motivator, too. Despite Rudolph's feeling that Britney had weakened his bargaining position, Fox agreed to pay her $15 million, the highest fee any judge had received to appear on a Simon Cowell talent show. Commentators speculated that she could ultimately net up to $200 million from new endorsement opportunities.

US shock jock Howard Stern felt it was not going to go well for Britney. 'I think Britney will sit there and eat a lollipop and wear a sexy outfit … I'll tune in to see what kind of train wreck she is, absolutely,' he said. This and other predictions of doom were boosted at a promotional event in New York to announce the new judging panel. Cowell remembered that there was a tense and 'stressful' atmosphere behind the scenes at the Beacon Theater, off Broadway. Britney and pop singer Demi Lovato were the two new judges who would line up alongside record company boss L. A. Reid and Cowell to complete the panel.

On the stage in front of the assembled advertisers, Reid said, 'This is the Rolls-Royce of TV right here.' When there were no signs of excitement or enthusiasm from the audience, Reid said, 'Oh, come on, this is Britney Spears!' This backfired and sparked only mild applause from the audience. As the judges were photographed in a marquee in Central Park later that day, one of the snappers trained his lens on Britney's heavily bitten and bloody fingernails.

It had been an awkward day, and things barely improved when on the suggestion of Britney the judges met up for dinner at ABC Kitchen in Lower Manhattan. Conversation was stilted, and Britney kept getting up and walking around the streets outside the restaurant, her nervous energy kicking in.

She remembered her first day, telling *Elle* she was 'extremely nervous' because she was 'having panic attack after panic attack'. However, she eventually realized she could be of use to the hopefuls simply by being 'honest' with them. Nevertheless, she still wanted to be gentle. 'Personally, I think that's the toughest part about being a judge on the X *Factor*,' she said. 'Most of them are still developing and it's hard to tell such young kids whether they have what it takes or not, so I try to be as protective as I can with their hopes and dreams.'

In time, Cowell hired his loyal sidekick Louis Walsh to cover for him. However, Walsh was initially blunt about his experience of working with Britney. Speaking to the *Irish Independent*, he recalled that 'after every few auditions' she would suddenly slump. 'They would literally have to stop the show and take her out because she was on so much medication and other stuff,' he said. 'I felt sorry for her.'

The Irishman added, 'Here she was, the biggest pop star on the planet, and she was just sitting there physically, but she wasn't there mentally. She had a lot of problems.' He continued, 'She was getting millions of dollars to do it, so why the f**k wouldn't she sit there?'

The reasons were not that mysterious, in truth. Britney was judging in 4,500-seater arenas that were packed with young audiences who had been whipped into hysteria. When she arrived on day one, the welcome had been deafening. For a concert this would be a good thing, but in this context it was challenging. She had to sit little more than an arm's length from the screaming crowd and then make judgements on young hopefuls' performances from an exposed position.

For Cowell, it was an enormously proud moment when, after the first contestant sang, he turned to his superstar judge and asked, 'Britney, what do you think?' He was still pinching himself that he had not only got her to sign for the show but then she had actually turned up. However, she looked uncomfortable, and within fifteen minutes she had got up and walked out of the auditorium.

Backstage, she was having a crisis of confidence. She asked Larry Rudolph if she had made the right decision signing up for the show. Should she, wondered Britney, be judging other people? The truth was that Britney had a shyness that belied her years in the spotlight. She also had a yearning for sincerity which meant that Britney, unlike some pop stars who would have sold their own grandparents for a space on the judging panel, believed she needed to deserve her spot. If she could not feel that way, she was not sure she wanted to continue.

There was a crisis on day one and it needed to be sorted – quickly. Cowell was approached by Rudolph, who asked the head judge to come and see her. When he arrived, she told him she thought she had made a mistake and that she wasn't the right person. He gave her a pep talk, telling Britney she had the right instincts and that no one was better positioned to judge talent than her. He gently reassured her and encouraged her to return to her seat. Rudolph, watching, was impressed with Cowell's people-management skills.

As for Cowell himself, he had expected teething problems at the start. He was realistic enough to know that Britney, who had never had to say 'no' to anyone in public before, would struggle with the tougher side of judging. He knew better than anyone how draining it could be to have people just behind you cheer and boo your every decision.

He also noted her shyness, particularly when she responded awkwardly to a fan shouting, 'I love you, Britney!' Cowell said, 'We all remember her with the snake around her neck and think, "She can't be shy." But she is.' He told Ellen DeGeneres: 'I kind of booked someone who couldn't talk, which is a bit of a problem when you want someone to judge.'

He told the production team that they would have to adapt around Britney, including her preference to regularly get up to stretch her legs or have a cigarette break. She continued to struggle and would eat alone during breaks rather than joining her fellow judges in the communal lounge.

The turning point came when Cowell dropped out of the auditions in Kansas and Louis Walsh stood in for him. When the Irishman arrived, the judges played a game that involved choosing a word they had to work into their next round of comments. Among the words were 'mountain', 'punk rock' and 'crocodile'. They had great fun as they found ways to drop them in, and Rudolph also noted how playful Walsh was with Britney.

She began to pull dramatic facial expressions, either of approval or disapproval. These made for great clips to show at the beginning of each episode and have since become popular online memes. When she was moved to sit next to L. A. Reid, she felt even more at ease. Before long, she was having banter with her fellow judges and even getting up to dance during auditions. She was refreshed from a holiday in Hawaii and had lost weight and enhanced her skin tone with a strict diet of chicken soup, salads and passion-fruit iced teas. Cowell biographer Tom Bower noted a change in mood from Britney as the auditions progressed. Eventually, he wrote, she was 'clearly more relaxed' and actually 'enjoying herself'.

When Carly Rose Sonenclar auditioned at the age of just thirteen, the moment felt very apt for Britney. The teen sang 'Feeling Good', and she did feel good as the judges cheered her through to the next round. She proceeded through the boot camp stage and landed in Britney's category for the judges' houses, which Britney would hold in Malibu. The proud judge advised the teenager to 'take your competitiveness [and] put it into your heart' as she performed. She sang 'Brokenhearted' for her mentor and Britney's guest judge will.i.am, and impressed them both. 'She's definitely possessed,' said Britney. Carly was put through to the live shows.

Among the songs she sang during the live shows were 'Over the Rainbow', 'Rolling in the Deep', 'Feeling Good', 'How Do I Live' (with LeAnn Rimes) and 'Hallelujah'. In the show's grand finale, she finished in second place behind Tate

Stevens. Likewise, as far as Cowell was concerned, Britney had been more of a runner-up than a winner herself. 'It's like having a dinner party,' he told MTV at the Television Critics Association panel. 'You invite people for dinner and sometimes it's a fun night, and other times it's not as fun as you hoped it would be.' It was harsh verdict from the man who had pulled out all the stops to hire her in the first place.

Reid was more positive but made a peculiar observation that he was surprised Britney was a music fan. 'Somehow I didn't connect her to loving music as much as she does,' he told *Billboard*. 'We went to a photoshoot once and she didn't know I was in the room. She was on her computer and she puts on Vanilla Ice's "Ice Ice Baby" and she just goes crazy, right? I loved it because [if] you don't know people, you don't know people. I love that she's really such a fan of music. I was a little bit surprised.' He added that Britney 'really is an artist and I don't know why I dismissed that'. Asked by TMZ if Britney could have won the competition had she ever competed, Reid said, 'If I was a judge, she would have won.' As for his experience alongside her on the show, he said, 'She's a lot of fun.'

For Britney, the show had opened up a new path for her and allowed the public to see a different side. It also brought her to something of a full circle: from the girl who entered talent shows to the woman who judged them. The worlds of reality television and music collided again in the aftermath of the show when her label, Jive, dissolved and was absorbed into RCA Records. The closure of Jive led to feverish speculation over where Britney would move to next.

Soon, said the *Hollywood Reporter*, L. A. Reid was trying to sign Britney to his Epic label. Reid was exploiting the close bond he and Britney had built up during the production of the *X Factor* to try to woo her to his company. 'Larry [Rudolph] and Jason [Trawick] will want to go where the money is,' a source told the publication, adding that Britney had developed 'a pretty good s**t-detector [where] if L. A. goes overboard, that could push her away'.

Barry Weiss, the former president of Jive who was with her during her heyday and had since moved to Universal's 'East Coast' labels, looking after artists including Justin Bieber, Kanye West and Rihanna, was also keen. He spoke of his 'fifteen-year history' with Britney while trying to tempt her to sign up with his new home. It was rumoured that both bidders were offering Britney up to $5 million per album.

Ultimately, she followed Jive into RCA, and it was that label that released her eighth album, *Britney Jean*. will.i.am was at the controls for the record and told *Billboard* he wanted to bring an autobiographical feel to it. Britney had recently broken up with Jason Trawick. The rumours that the couple had once been married were untrue, but the break was nevertheless upsetting enough to provide Britney with plenty of raw emotion to draw upon. 'I wanted to just go to lunch for two months, which is totally different from how you typically do it,' will.i.am explained.

I said, 'Let's talk about what you're excited about.
Let's talk about things you've done in your career,
what you're happy about. Let's talk about spending

time with your kids, let's talk about your break-up. Let's talk about how now you're single, how independent you might feel.' We started talking about all that stuff. So, I said, 'Do you mind if I write this down? I don't mean to impose, but I want to interview you. I need this to create a filter.'

Elijah Blake, one of the songwriting team, remarked that she was 'definitely trying to push the envelope' by 'playing with new textures and stomping on new grounds and genres'. Suitably, Britney said it was the most personal album she had put out.

'Alien' renders the existential loneliness of celebrity life, offering an intimacy that had gone missing all too often in recent collections. 'Work Bitch' has become one of Britney's most iconic tracks; the EDM song is as consumerist and cheap as they come but brilliantly so. The club banger sees her suggest the secret to her success, and whether people find it shallow or a more meaningful encouragement for her fans to work hard for what they want, it is exhilarating and impossible to ignore.

'Perfume' is a gentler, synth pop ballad with a strong 1980s feel. Lyrically, the song is built around themes of jealousy and suspicion in a relationship. Hinting that it was influenced by her split with Trawick, she said it is 'incredibly special to me because it hits close to home, and I think the story is relatable to everyone'. Everyone, she added, has 'been through an insecure moment in a relationship that's left them vulnerable and I think this song captures that'.

Speaking to Associated Press, she said, 'I think it will make girls not feel alone in this situation. When they're alone in their room and they broke up with their boyfriend, they have a song they can go to and listen to that just makes them feel better about themselves.'

'It Should Be Easy', where she duets with will.i.am, is about how love 'shouldn't be complicated' but all too often is. Britney dares to dream of a bright, normal future with a man who's stolen her heart. 'Tik Tik Boom' has been described as 'sex drenched' and 'Body Ache' is a love song to nightclubs. 'Til It's Gone' covers that universally relatable theme of not fully appreciating what you had in your relationship until it was over. Meanwhile, 'Passenger' deals with control and 'Chillin' With You' goes almost country, quite a leap from the big bangers Britney had become associated with. 'Don't Cry' opens with unexpected spaghetti western whistling, and the song sees a strong vocal shift from Britney as she sings about not giving in to the heartbreak of a failed relationship. The deluxe album included four more tracks, including a mix of 'Perfume'.

On this album, Britney was barely a vocalist. The theories as to why this was the case ranged from the cynical – that she had rushed the album to promote her Vegas shows – to the conspiratorial – that her label was road-testing how little involvement a pop star could have in an album. Then there was speculation that she was losing her voice. All just another day in the wild relationship between Britney and the media.

Billboard described the album as a 'transitional record

[as] her first album released in her thirties' and compared it with her third studio album, *Britney*. *Entertainment Weekly* said that in 'just ten tidy songs [it] brings us closer than ever before to that distant dreamer'. *Rolling Stone* felt it was a 'concept album about the loneliness of pop life' and that with a 'high-profile broken engagement behind her, Brit gets personal and drops her most bummed-out music ever'. *Spin* said it saw her 'go blanker than usual', while Michael Cragg of the *Guardian* complained of 'a handful of anonymous, emotion-sapping EDM stompers' and gave the album just two out of five stars.

The *Los Angeles Times* thought the album was Britney on 'autopilot', with Randall Roberts saying it is 'marked with so many sleights of hand, dubious lyrics and bombastic but boringly simple melodies that the too-rare levitation of its better moments seems an animation trick'. In a harsh verdict, he wrote that 'whatever unique skills Spears once had – what were they again, anyway? – *Britney Jean* suggests she better prepare herself for the reality that she's losing them fast'. The paper gave just 1.5 stars out of four.

The *Chicago Tribune* said, 'The hype about her most "personal" album yet begins with the album title ... which promotes a sense of intimacy that the songs never quite deliver.' And *The New York Times* was more cutting, describing *Britney Jean* as 'about as personal as an airline preboarding announcement'. Jon Pareles wrote that on recent outings, Britney had been 'brazenly artificial' but 'also vibrant, and ... held a multitude of cultural implications about desire, technology, stardom and pop calculation', whereas on *Britney Jean*, 'the fun leaches out while the calculation stays obvious'.

The *Atlantic* described the album as 'dull' and 'her most disappointing release yet'. Meanwhile, the *Daily Telegraph*'s big-hitter reviewer Neil McCormick wrote that the 'banal' album 'continues the striptease of Britney's career', complaining that 'behind each discarded veil there is just another veil, an insubstantial gauze masking teams of (presumably unphotogenic) producers, writers, stylists and sloganeers'.

In a slip in performance, the album debuted at number four on the US *Billboard* 200, with first-week sales of 107,000 copies. It was her lowest peaking and lowest selling record in the United States. In the UK, it reached no higher than number thirty-four after initially selling just 13,000 copies. Her lack of promotional activity around the album did not help, but there was also a sense that the public was tiring of Britney.

There was no album-specific tour for *Britney Jean*, but she had some ambitious live plans of a slightly different kind. Rumours of Britney undertaking a Vegas residency had swirled around for years. She was linked to various venues in the city, including SLS Las Vegas and the Colosseum at Caesars Palace. Speaking to *Shape*, Britney added fuel to the fire of speculation by saying she was lining up some performances, adding, 'They won't be simple – they'll be a massive party from start to finish. And to pull this off, I have to be in top condition and running at full speed.'

When it was finally time to announce the shows, which

would take place at Planet Hollywood, Britney broke the news in style. She made the announcement on *Good Morning America* with a live helicopter stunt in Las Vegas. More than a thousand of her fans had gathered in the desert, and they held signs that combined to show a picture of Spears as she circled in a helicopter high above. 'This is such a sweet thing to do,' she said. 'I don't even know what to say. I'm speechless. This is shocking.'

She said she had been training as much as five hours per day for the show – a typically high level of preparation for Britney The 2013 shows started with a strong sequence: 'Work Bitch', 'Womanizer' and '3'. Reporting on the 'sold-out crowd of A-list celebrities, reporters, die-hard fans and family members', Danielle Genet of ABC News said the opening night was full of 'fervour'. Meanwhile, *USA Today* writer Marco della Cava wrote, 'Spears stomped into town with a twenty-one-hit salute to her fifteen years of dance confections that artfully melded spectacle with stagecraft.'

Writing for MTV News, Sophie Schillaci said Britney 'delivered on her signature style of larger-than-life production, blaring beats and rapid-fire dance moves, whirling through seven costume changes and even a couple of wig changes'. On the question of whether Britney was singing live, *Billboard*'s reviewer Keith Caulfield wrote of the thrill of hearing Spears 'breathing into the microphone'. Nevertheless, said the *Los Angeles Times*, the residency was a 'gamble'. The conservatorship had always felt like something of a gamble, too, and that particular punt was beginning to break apart.

Chapter Nine

I'M A SLAVE 4 U

It was an illness in the Spears family that led to the unravelling of the conservatorship arrangement. When Jamie ruptured his colon in November 2018, leading to his immediate hospitalization, Britney quickly announced the cancellation of her second Domination residency at the Park MGM resort in Las Vegas.

In a statement she said, 'I am dedicating my focus and energy to care for my family. We have a very special relationship and I want to be with my family at this time just like they have always been there for me. Thank you to all my fans for your continued love and support during this time. I apologize for any inconvenience this may have caused and I look forward to the time when I can be back on stage performing for all of you.'

This message of familial unity somewhat went against the flow of Britney's life, as would become clear in the months ahead. In May 2019, she attended her annual conservatorship hearing, with a source telling CNN that she requested to end the arrangement. Mother and daughter arrived hand in hand, a symbolic moment. Earlier that week, Lynne had filed to be kept abreast of Britney's medical conditions.

Soon, Jamie was back in court, asking to reinstate himself

and Andrew Wallet, an attorney who once helped oversee Britney's finances, as her co-conservators. In 2008, a court had named Jamie the permanent conservator of her person and Wallet the permanent co-conservator of her estate. However, Wallet had relinquished his powers in March 2019. The lawyer had said in a court notice: 'The conservatorship is engaged in numerous ongoing business activities requiring immediate attention and it therefore is in the best interest of the conservatee that the acceptance of Wallet's resignation and the issuance of amended letters of conservatorship of the estate occur immediately and without delay.'

Jodi Montgomery – a licensed conservator – had taken Jamie's place on a temporary basis while he was unwell. However, Jamie's bid to regain control did not sit well with Britney. Her court-appointed attorney, Samuel D. Ingham III, submitted a filing in Los Angeles stating that Britney was 'strongly opposed' to having her father return as the sole conservator of her affairs and finances and instead 'strongly prefers to have a qualified corporate fiduciary appointed to serve in this role'. This reprised the message that had been emerging from the cracks in the Spears team for some time: Britney's priority was removing Jamie from the arrangement.

Britney herself entered a mental health facility in the spring of 2019. After she was taken home, a source told E! News: 'It was her decision to leave, but she will still be monitored from home.' She took to Instagram to try to clear up the story. 'I wanted to say hi, because things that are being said have just gotten out of control!!! Wow!!! There's rumors, death threats to my family and my team, and just so many crazy things being said. I am trying to take a moment for myself, but everything that's happening is just making it harder for me. Don't believe everything you read and hear,' she wrote. 'You may not know this about me, but I am strong, and stand up for what I want! Your love and dedication is amazing, but what I need right now is a little bit of privacy to deal with all the hard things that life is throwing my way. If you could do that, I would be forever grateful.'

Back in 2016, while promoting her new album *Glory*, Britney reportedly attempted to make a public statement about the conservatorship arrangement. A PopCrush contributor who was in the audience for a recording of the *Jonathan Ross Show* said Britney addressed the situation openly for the first time: 'Okay, so I have this conservatorship. I've been under this conservatorship for three years and I felt like a lot of decisions were made for me, so I wanted [*Glory*] to be my baby and I've been really strategic about it,' she reportedly said. However, the alleged quote was cut when the show aired.

With her new album, Britney was aiming to surprise listeners. Indeed, a 2020 cover art update hammered the idea home, featuring a scantily clad Britney lying in a desert setting with chains alongside her. The message was clear and glamorously rendered. Executive producer Karen Kwak said that Britney 'wanted to do things that were fresh and unexpected this time'. Kwak added: 'There was never a moment where she was given a song, and anybody said, "This is a hit. You have to sing it." Britney pursued the songs she wanted to do for herself. She came up with concepts and melodies. It's her baby. It's like being an athlete. If you're doing it that much, you're getting yourself into shape. She was always ready to work during the album sessions.'

Notable tracks included 'Do You Wanna Come Over?' This flirty, cheeky, teasing track delivers musically what its title alludes to. Nobody should be alone if they don't have to be, she insists. 'Make Me' is about what happens after the flirtation, and rarely has she sounded so sexual. 'Clumsy', which felt like an Ariana Grande song, is also about sex but the most awkward moments it can create. '"Clumsy" is really cool, this was done in the middle of the process of the record and I wanted something really funky and this track came out of really nowhere and we brought it home,' she told SiriusXM.

Where 'Make Me' and 'Clumsy' had been a bit naughty, 'Slumber Party' blows the doors off. She sings the praises of sex and making sex tapes, using double entendres while mentioning one-night stands, the joy of sleepovers with friends and teenage games. It sounded like it could have sat on her 2003 album *In the Zone*. 'Just Like Me' sets out as if it is going to be a Taylor Swift-like song but soon takes a more electro direction. 'Love Me Down' oozes with attitude and sass, with a reggae feel. 'Hard to Forget Ya' feels more like a track for a band than a solo artist, with a comparatively soft vocal. However, its chant chorus is one for the fans to join in with. And 'What You Need' is pure cabaret, ending with Britney saying, 'That was fun.' She sounds pleasantly surprised.

After some savage notices for her recent albums, Britney

received some positive reviews for *Glory*. Neil McCormick from the *Daily Telegraph* said, 'Every track sounds like a single,' and the *Los Angeles Times* said her vocals were 'a vast improvement' and helped make *Glory* 'such a good time'. *Rolling Stone*, too, was enamoured of her vocal performance, saying, 'She hasn't played around with her vocals so cleverly since the "Toxic" days.'

Vice gave the album an A- rating but in language that reeked of misogyny and condescension remarked that *Glory*'s 'fast-tracked eroticism is an unprecedented achievement even for this longtime professional sex toy'. *Idolator* praised her to the hilt for sounding 'more lucid, engaged and front-and-center than she's been in years'. Nolan Feeney from *Entertainment Weekly* lauded the material as sounding 'like glimpses of the real Britney – her musical tastes, her voice – imperfections and all'.

The New York Times noted that the pop charts 'are now crowded with younger performers who have studied her the way Ms Spears studied Madonna' and suggested that her strategy with the album was 'relentless and unambiguous: stick to sexy'. Jon Pareles concluded that *Glory* showed Britney 'can still only present herself as that most generic pop commodity: a sexpot'. The *Boston Globe*'s assessment was more upbeat: *Glory* sounded like Britney was having fun again. The *Guardian* called it 'a triumphant return'.

It began at number three on the US *Billboard* 200, shifting 112,000 album-equivalent units in its first week. It topped the charts in the Czech Republic, Ireland, Italy and Taiwan and also peaked within the top ten of charts in another twenty countries. She bounced back in the UK, reaching number two – her highest charting album since *Blackout*. In Germany, it reached number three, the highest chart position there since *In the Zone*.

To support the album's release, Britney gave an interview to *Marie Claire* magazine in the UK. She revealed that the Vegas shows, which had physically demanding choreography, had taken it out of her. She said her little sister had encouraged her to eat more to make up for this. 'She's always trying to get me to eat,' said Britney. 'I never ate sushi until a year or so ago. I thought the idea of raw fish was horrible. Then we had a day in a hotel in Vegas and she ordered up every single bit of sushi they had and we sat there just eating everything. Now I'm hooked.'

With family on her mind, Britney also spoke about her relationship with her two sons. She painted a picture of how they kept her grounded and offered a welcome respite from the harsh focus of fame. 'My boys don't care if everything isn't perfect, they don't judge me,' she told the magazine. 'If anything, when I'm all dressed up they aren't happy because it usually means I'm going to work. I've been through a lot and I've got to this point where I'm feeling good about being single. The best relationship I've ever had is with my boys.'

Cementing this family theme, a former boyfriend told *The New York Times* that Britney's relationship with her sons was her priority and the health of that relationship suggested her conservatorship could be lifted. 'If anyone knew the real Britney, they would know that she would rather be remembered for being the great mother she is rather than the artist she is,' said David Lucado, who dated her in 2013. 'And if anyone could see her interactions with her kids, they would know that there is no need for a conservatorship over Britney's personal life.' Britney might not have been speaking much about her situation, but others were beginning to plant seeds in the public mind.

Those seeds would soon start to sprout and grow. Meanwhile, her status and progress were being measured by a court investigator, who was assigned to file reports on Britney's progress once every other year. Critics of the conservatorship arrangement pointed out it involved a lot of payments going out. For instance, reported *The New York Times*, her chief advocate, Samuel D. Ingham III, was awarded more than $2 million in fees for his work on her behalf between 2008 and 2016. Additionally, $6.9 million was paid from the estate to the conservators and other lawyers who had helped manage her affairs under the arrangement at that stage.

Legal papers obtained by a Britney fan podcast stated, 'The conservatee's business activities have greatly accelerated, due to her increased wellbeing and her capacity to be more engaged in furthering her career activities. The next several years promise to be very lucrative for the conservatorship estate.' The legal documents later added, 'This conservatorship should be viewed more as a hybrid business model.'

Where would be the motivation to end the arrangement while it was helping people trouser money, some began to wonder. 'As long as she is bringing in so much money and as long as the lawyers and conservators are getting paid, there is little incentive to end it,' Elaine Renoire, president of the National Association to Stop Guardian Abuse advocacy group, told *The NYT*. 'Usually, the conservatorship just keeps going unless the conservatee makes a fuss or the family does.'

The paper reported that Jamie took in about $130,000 a year as a conservator and was also reimbursed for the rent on an office he used. His bills were reviewed and approved by the judge. He had sought only modest increases over the years, though he also requested 1.5 per cent of gross revenues from the performances and merchandising tied to Britney's Las Vegas show. The court, Britney and her court-appointed lawyer signed off on it.

So, what was this work? According to his court filings, it included 'overseeing and coordinating Britney's [redacted], business, costuming, personal, household stuff, and legal matters (touching upon entertainment, music, other business opportunities, family law issues, the litigation, trial and/ or resolution of other disputes, and ongoing litigation and conservatorship matters)'.

Meanwhile, she had a new ally in her life in the form of Sam Asghari, who she met on the set of the promo video for 'Slumber Party'. He played an attractive man in a suit who watches as Britney suggestively laps up spilt milk. However, he later told *GQ* 'it was the humbleness' that attracted him to her. 'She was very humble and she had a beautiful soul.' He told *Men's Health* magazine he 'had butterflies', and when he tried to break the ice he almost ruined his chances thanks to a questionable joke. 'She said, "Hi, I'm Britney," and I said, "I'm sorry, what's your name again?"' he told the magazine. 'I tried to be funny. I don't think anybody got it.' As for Britney, she said, 'I found his number in my bag. I was like, "He is really cute. This guy is really cute,"' she recalled during a January 2017 radio interview. 'So, then I called him, and ever since then, he is just a really fun, funny person.'

Fortunately, they were able to bond initially over a shared love of sushi. From there, the couple soon found common ground on their love of sports and outdoors activity. He had to accept that his partner was usually going to emerge on top. 'She has cat-like reflexes, and she's really, really good,' he said. 'When we play tennis, it gets competitive and most of the time, well, ping pong, she beats me every time. She's really good at basketball.'

All couples have to work out how they are going to manage their finances, but this conversation can be more vexed when one of them has a fortune and the other does not. 'I am dating a girl that's very expensive, she has an expensive taste but I do try to incorporate my lifestyle to her as well,' he said. To have a man in her life who looked at things other than her ability to generate money was to prove enormously healthy for Britney. It was just what the doctor had ordered.

Her confidence was beginning to grow, and she dared to dream of a future of more freedom. In a recording later published by *Rolling Stone*, she said, 'I basically want my life back. I want to be able to drive my car. I want to be able to live in my house by myself. I want to be able to say who's going to be my bodyguard.' Then, in a voicemail left for her lawyers, she claimed she had been 'threatened' by her father. She wanted her legal team to reassure her that 'everything will be fine with the process of you guys taking care of everything – that things will stay the same as far as my custodial time'.

As Britney's confidence grew, so did public awareness. These tandem developments would put the issue directly on the map. Media coverage began to become weighted significantly in Britney's favour. There was growing scepticism among commentators. 'Some people worry that Britney's family are using her for all the wrong reasons,' Michelle Lee, editor of showbiz magazine *In Touch Weekly*, said. She added, 'It is hard to see whether the people around her are there for the right reasons.'

It is easy to portray Jamie as the baddie in the conservatorship story. Indeed, a significant chunk of the media has gleefully taken this stance, and comments about his perceived greed became commonplace. However, it is more complex than that, and at this stage it is helpful to reflect on two key details of Jamie's life to try to understand what might have been going on in his head.

According to a local paper, Jamie's mother died by suicide on the grave of her infant son. Emma Jean Spears had battled with depression for nine years and attempted suicide on three separate occasions before she finally took her life. The death was covered on the front page of the local newspaper, *Kentwood News*, and the local community was stunned – none more so than Jamie, who was then thirteen.

Then, four years later, Jamie survived a car accident that killed a football teammate. His inability to save either his mother or his friend might have haunted him, even though there is no suggestion that he should have been able to save either.

There had also been some serious scares in the early years of his son Bryan's life. Bryan was born with an infection on his lung and almost died within hours of being born, as he lacked the immunity to fight it easily. His parents felt helpless.

Lynne also faced tragedy before Britney was born. One day, a piece of tractor equipment fell on her brother, Sonny. As he moaned with pain, she drove him to the hospital. On the way, there was a tragic accident. Writing in her memoir, she said the roads were 'slick with rain', and as she turned a corner she saw two boys on their bikes. She realized that, however hard she hit the breaks, she would hit one of the cyclists. She did, and twelve-year-old Anthony Winters died. As Lynne arrived at hospital, she heard what she described as the 'blood-curdling screams' of the boy's mother. Lynne was never charged, and the boy's death was deemed to be accidental.

As Lynne and Jamie watched their daughter's life spiral out of control, it would not have been surprising if they revisited these tragedies of their past and felt determined that, this time at least, they would save a life that seemed to be nearing a tragic and early end. Debbie Sanders Cross, Jamie's first wife, who remained a friend, told *The New York Times* that she believed his own 'very difficult upbringing' had influenced his perspective. 'I really think that's why he's trying to be so protective of Britney,' she said.

With the ghosts of his past haunting him, Jamie moved in to take control of Britney's life. And with Lynne having her own tragic memories, each of Britney's parents had reason to be enormously anxious. Additionally, for those who have never faced the level of attention and wealth that came Britney and her family's way so suddenly, it can be hard to realize how terrifying both can become.

In truth, none of their lives would ever be the same again, as Britney's eventful life entered its most controversial chapter to date. For Jamie, the coming years would be tricky as the spotlight increasingly focused on the conservatorship and his role in it. Britney and her closest relatives had grown accustomed to living in the public glare, but the intensity – and in many ways the hostility – of that glare was unusual. As Britney rose to fame, the public loved everything about her. Then for a while people were concerned about her. Now, many people around the world were also angry on her behalf.

Core to the sceptical attention was a contradiction at the heart of Britney's life. In the years following the conservatorship, she flourished professionally. However, she kept a low profile, granting few interviews, all of which were micro-managed. Reporters said they had been forced to jump through hoops of bureaucracy to get any access at all. However, her breathless work schedule – albums, concerts, live television, endorsement deals, reality television – seemed impossible for the person described in the conservatorship terms to perform. Was she really so vulnerable that she was unable to function on her own, or was she a brave workaholic? What was the truth?

Chapter Ten

FREE BRITNEY!

Social media has given the fan bases of pop stars an influence that never existed before the digital age. Fans around the world could unite at the click of a mouse and make their numbers felt. The dramatic success of the likes of Justin Bieber and One Direction are, in large part, thanks to the power of social media that did not exist for the pop idols of previous generations. Just as these online masses could help put a star on a pedestal, they could also defend them when the chips were down.

Nowhere has this been better seen than with the #FreeBritney movement. Indeed, the campaign is perhaps the most powerful example of fan power to date. For several years, Britney's fans bubbled up pressure for their heroine to be liberated from her conservatorship. They probed the details of the arrangement, combed through her social media posts for clues and browsed legal documents with a fine-toothed comb. Never underestimate the power of dedicated fans, particularly when combined with the march of technology. The pressure they built simmered up higher and higher, and then, in 2019, it started to boil over.

More than anyone, it was the hosts of podcast *Britney's Gram* who turned up the heat. Each week, comedians Tess

Barker and Barbara Gray humorously discussed and dissected Britney's Instagram posts. 'The comedy of the podcast, we thought, would derive from us taking something so mundane incredibly seriously,' Barker told the *Los Angeles Times*. 'So we really intended it to be, maybe not quite satire, but a comedic kind of take, because we thought, "How ridiculous to do a deep dive on someone's Instagram feed."'

Soon, though, the project became more serious when the pair started to feel that all was not well with Britney's postings. 'There was a certain *je ne sais quoi* in those posts that drew us in,' said Barker. 'We didn't know what we were looking at yet, but something was off. And I think that is sort of what compelled us to examine it so closely.' That closer examination was to prove a force that helped unravel the entire arrangement.

In a pivotal episode, the hosts reported that they had been contacted by a whistleblower with a voicemail message that alleged Britney was in a mental health facility against her will and that she was there because of punitive measures being taken by her father. 'What happened with the voicemail … I mean, we've been in the entertainment industry long enough that, at this point, I tend to believe rumors that I hear going around for a long time,' said Barker. 'I think we learned from things like the Bill Cosby situation and the Harvey Weinstein situation. Those are not things that happen overnight. Those were things that they're whispering about for years. And so that sort of felt like what happened with the voicemail.'

The lid may not have been entirely blown off, but a significant crack had been opened. For years, many of

Britney's fans had been suspicious about what was going on behind the polished façade of her image. What was this conservatorship and how exactly did it work? Was their heroine being protected for her own good, or was she being oppressed and exploited?

When the voicemail was revealed, it felt as if all their doubts had been confirmed and all their questions had been answered. A protest was held in April 2019, with around two dozen fans gathering outside West Hollywood City Hall with signs bearing slogans such as, 'The truth will set her free'. Gray, of the *Britney's Gram* podcast, said, 'So the voicemail came out, [and] we had a West Hollywood rally just randomly – twenty, thirty people maybe.' The campaigners, many wearing Britney merchandise, gathered peacefully and played her music. A handful of reporters turned up and covered the protest as if it were a joke. They would not be laughing for long.

The *Britney's Gram* hosts started a new, more hard-hitting investigative series called *Toxic: The Britney Spears Story*. They gained access to people close to Britney's inner circle. 'A common narrative emerged,' wrote Tess Barker for the *i*. 'Britney Spears had, since being placed under conservatorship in 2008, been cut off from loved ones.' They heard that Britney faced restrictions 'on what she could eat [and] when and if she could leave the house'. Barker wrote that 'many someone elses decided how her fortune – which she'd been actively growing through near-constant work – would be spent'. A source told them: 'You guys are on to something.'

Suddenly, the Free Britney movement was exploding into life.

The movement brought together many Britney fans and became about so much more than its essential aim. It drew attention to wider issues and acted as something of a personal salvation for many in its number. One member, Wu, told the *Framing Britney Spears* documentary: 'There were people like myself who felt like they didn't fit in; I think there was some wanting to aspire to that image. We know now Britney wasn't perfect. Britney had to navigate being told who she could be and what she could do. I think that story of control and identity resonates.' Another member, quoted in Jennifer Otter Bickerdike's *Being Britney*, said, 'This is so much deeper than just Britney Spears, the pop star, this is a human rights issue at the root of it; it's a women's rights issue ... I do not trust the system – not that I ever did – but I certainly don't now.'

These fascinating campaigners were waking up and making plenty of noise. Then, *The New York Times* reported that Britney had confirmed to the court during a closed-door hearing in May 2019 that she had been forced to go to a mental health facility against her will. She reportedly saw it as punishment for making an objection during a rehearsal for her Las Vegas residency, which she said she once performed with a 104-degree fever. However, Jamie and his legal team have firmly denied claims that he has mismanaged Britney's life and career.

Quickly, the campaign went from a fringe joke to a vibrant, mainstream concern. For many of its most committed members, the battle became all-consuming. They arranged rallies, marketed and promoted their cause online and travelled across the US to attend protests. Some even went so far as moving house so they could be nearer the heart of the action in Los Angeles. This was a dedicated crew who were willing to go the extra mile(s) to make noise on behalf of their hero.

Yet their roots may have stretched back further than some thought. Although received wisdom has it that the *Britney's Gram* podcast and its findings were the springboard for the #FreeBritney movement itself, some commentators trace its history back as far as 2009. A Spears fan site, BreatheHeavy.com, started a 'Free Britney' campaign against the conservatorship from its beginning. When the website's owner, Jordan Miller, heard that Britney's father had taken away her mobile phone, he wrote, 'Open your eyes! Free Britney!'

Soon after, he says he received an irate call from Jamie, who threatened to have the website taken down; Miller had scored an own-goal by reproducing Britney's lyrics on the website, which opened him up to the risk of a copyright lawsuit. The fan was not impressed. 'In my opinion, it's not about lyrics,' he told the *Independent*. 'It's because I was speaking out about an injustice, and they didn't like that, and they wanted to control everything about Britney, including entities that they didn't technically own.'

Similarly, the more recent #FreeBritney campaign claimed it had been probed by her father. According to reports, a security firm hired by Jamie investigated the group. It sent secret infiltrators to their rallies and drew up a 'threat assessment report' of the fans. In response to controversy, a lawyer for the firm Black Box said it was 'proud of their work in keeping Ms Spears safe' and had operated 'within professional, ethical and legal bounds'.

Nonetheless, Jamie Spears had little doubt or nuance when it came to his feelings over the #FreeBritney movement. Speaking to the *New York Post*'s Page Six, he said the movement was 'a joke', adding, 'All these conspiracy theorists don't know anything. The world doesn't have a clue. It's up to the court of California to decide what's best for my daughter. It's no one else's business. I love my daughter. I love all my kids. But this is our business. It's private.'

These were defiant words. What seemed to have particularly enraged him was the perception that he was using the arrangement to skim money from Britney's earnings. 'I have to report every nickel and dime spent to the court every year,' he said. 'How the hell would I steal something?' He added that the campaign to end the conservatorship was having a rough impact on many involved. 'People are being stalked and targeted with death threats,' he said. 'It's horrible. We don't want those kinds of fans.'

Indeed, Britney's former lawyer later stated he did not think Jamie was indulging in any financial skulduggery. 'Jamie's a weird guy, he's a control freak,' Adam Streisand said. 'But I don't see him as some sort of criminal mastermind in this.' This was not an assessment that Jamie emerged from spotlessly, but it was another refutation of the allegation he found most incendiary.

There were also growing signs of disharmony between Jamie and his grandsons. Jayden went on the attack in a post on Instagram Live, saying, 'He's a pretty big d**k. He's pretty f**king gay as s**t. He can go die.' Not the most loving words a grandfather has ever heard from a grandson. However, Federline's family lawyer ultimately tried to play down the incident, describing it as 'the result of a thirteen-year-old acting like a thirteen-year-old'.

More poised and potent was the involvement of Britney's mother, Lynne, as the #FreeBritney campaign grew in size. She reportedly 'liked' comments on Instagram that used the 'Free Britney' hashtag, a powerful intervention. When a Britney fan posted that positive comments under Britney's posts were being deleted, Lynne responded that she had noticed some of her comments were deleted, too. 'I know you are a true fan and love her so thank you for pointing this out because I have had others say the same,' she wrote. Then Britney's brother, Bryan, claimed on a podcast that his sister had wanted the conservatorship to end for 'quite some time', adding, 'She's always wanted to get out of it.'

Conspiracy theories around Britney's social media had grown in tandem with the rise of the #FreeBritney movement. Eagle-eyed fans would comb through every detail of her Instagram posts, searching for evidence that she was not in control of her postings or that she was sending out coded messages to the world. When one of her posts featured an emoticon, rather than an emoji, fans believed the post had been made by someone other than their pop idol.

Similarly, when she posted a Scrabble board with the

letters jumbled up, some fans believed they spotted the word 'quit' spelled backwards and interpreted this as a cry for help. When she made a post about people needing to care more for the 'lonely kid in the cafeteria', for some fans the issue was beyond doubt: Britney was calling out to them.

They got to work trying to reach out to their idol. A follower asked Britney to wear a yellow shirt in her next video if she needed help. Sure enough, in her following post she was wearing a yellow top. Over on Twitter, a fan asked Britney to post an image of doves if she was in peril. Britney posted an Austrian painting that included five doves. As these incidents caused a storm on and beyond social media, Britney's team told the *New Yorker*: 'She's not a prisoner with no rights.' Later, her social media manager remarked of Britney that 'she is literally just living her life and trying to have fun on Instagram'. She insisted that some fans were conjuring up 'inaccurate theories' over what was going on.

Nevertheless, support for Britney was growing. The American Civil Liberties Union tweeted about the pop star's ongoing legal battle with her father, writing, 'People with disabilities have a right to lead self-directed lives and retain their civil rights. If Britney Spears wants to regain her civil liberties and get out of her conservatorship, we are here to help her.'

Then, in a filing which objected to her father constantly sealing details of the cases, Britney acknowledged the #FreeBritney campaign for the first time. 'Britney's conservatorship has attracted an unprecedented level of scrutiny from mainstream media and social media alike,' the filing read. 'Far from being a conspiracy theory or a "joke", as James reportedly told the media, in large part this scrutiny is a reasonable and even predictable result of James' aggressive use of the sealing procedure over the years to minimize the amount of meaningful information made available to the public.' The filing also included the dramatic and borderline threatening statement: 'The world is watching.' In a boost for the campaign, the document said, 'Britney welcomes and appreciates the informed support of her many fans.'

Two months later, Britney's lawyer said she wouldn't perform as long as Jamie was a conservator, adding, 'My client has informed me that she is afraid of her father,' NBC News reported. The stakes were being raised and the moves were becoming bolder. The judge didn't remove Jamie, but she did add financial company Bessemer Trust as a co-conservator. Meanwhile, Jamie was actually bidding to extend the scope of the arrangement in court. He requested that it allow him to still serve as Britney's guardian when she was in Louisiana – and potentially Florida and Hawaii – which had not previously been specified.

However uncomfortable Jamie felt about the #FreeBritney campaign in its early months, he hadn't seen anything yet. *Framing Britney Spears* – a 2021 documentary released by *The New York Times* – was widely watched and reported on and made for very uncomfortable viewing for Spears' father. Examining her rise to fame, it included some incendiary remarks from former Jive Records marketing executive Kim Kaiman: 'The only thing Jamie ever said to me was, "My daughter's gonna be so rich, she's gonna buy me a boat,"' Kaiman claimed.

The documentary also deftly portrayed the seeming contradiction between the premise of the conservatorship – that Britney was unable to manage her own affairs – and the fact that she continued working full-time after it was imposed. Was she incapable or not, viewers were left wondering. Her long-time family friend and former assistant Felicia Culotta said she was as confused as anyone about the conservatorship arrangement, 'especially for somebody Britney's age and somebody capable of so much that I know first-hand she's capable of'.

Variety said the film provided 'a sort of pocket portrait of a person for whom freedom has been denied and for whom that denial comes as no surprise'. *NME*'s Nick Levine described it as a 'heartbreakingly human story that still lacks a happy ending'. However, Fiona Sturges of the *Independent* said the documentary was 'lacking in journalistic rigour'.

The documentary was welcomed by the #FreeBritney movement. 'It did such a great job of reframing the way we look at Britney and creating some sympathy for her and showing how wrong it was the way she was treated. It showed these people how we are fighting for her,' said Leanne Simmons, a #FreeBritney organizer who was featured in the documentary. 'This is a human rights issue.'

In the wake of the broadcast, the stakes and tensions rose even further. The feeling was strong that something big was about to change. Britney's boyfriend, Sam Asghari, wrote on Instagram that Jamie is a 'total d**k' who tried to control their relationship. As the claims flew back and forth, Jamie's lawyers alleged that Britney was able to end the conservatorship at 'any time' but had chosen not to.

After the documentary aired, Britney made several veiled references to her situation on Instagram. In one post, she wrote, 'I am taking the time to learn and be a normal person. I love simply enjoying the basics of everyday life!!! ... Remember, no matter what we think we know about a person's life, it is nothing compared to the actual person living behind the lens!!'

In a since-deleted Instagram post, Britney wrote that she felt 'embarrassed' watching the beginning of *Framing Britney Spears*. 'It takes a lot of strength to TRUST the universe with your real vulnerability cause I've always been so judged ... insulted ... and embarrassed by the media ... and I still am till this day!!!!' she wrote. 'I didn't watch the [whole] documentary but from what I did see of it, I was embarrassed by the light they put me in ... I cried for two weeks and well ... I still cry sometimes!!!!'

A month after the documentary was broadcast, Ingham filed to take Jamie out of the conservatorship completely and hand the full responsibility to previous stand-in caretaker Jodi Montgomery. Then, the stakes were raised when Ingram stated at the Los Angeles Superior Court: 'Britney wants to address the court directly.' The voice that billions had heard sing had nevertheless remained largely silent during the public conversation about the guardianship. Now, she was going to speak at last. Indeed, onlookers hoped she would 'sing like a bird' and bring the whole arrangement tumbling down.

In June 2021, the issue blew up into mainstream attention when Britney told a Los Angeles judge: 'I just want my life back.' It was the culmination of years of growing drama as she appeared and gave her side of the story. In a twenty-three-minute livestream testimony, she told the court she had been drugged, forced to work against her will and prevented from removing her birth control device under the legal arrangement that had ruled her life for more than thirteen years. 'I truly believe this conservatorship is abusive,' she told the court. 'I don't feel like I can live a full life.' She also alleged at the hearing that her conservators were 'abusive' and 'bullied' her.

She took the court behind the scenes of her preparations for the 2018 Las Vegas shows, painting a picture of herself as a more than able woman. 'I was basically directing most of the show,' she said. 'I actually did most of the choreography, meaning I taught my dancers my new choreography myself. I take everything I do very seriously. There's tons of video with me at rehearsals. I wasn't good – I was great. I led a room of sixteen new dancers in rehearsals.' Again, the contradiction was clear: Britney was being asked to work hard and with some managerial authority ... while being held in a conservatorship that cast her as a helpless naïf.

She pressed on, saying of her father that 'the control he had over someone as powerful as me – he loved the control to hurt his own daughter 100,000 per cent. He loved it.' She spoke of working seven days a week, with 'no days off' and said, 'In California, the only similar thing to this is called sex trafficking.' Britney added that her 'precious body, who has worked for my dad for the past f**king thirteen years, trying to be so good and pretty' was exhausted.

She said that for years she had 'lied and told the whole world, "I'm okay and I'm happy." It's a lie. I thought just maybe if I said that enough maybe I might become happy, because I've been in denial. I've been in shock. I am traumatized. You know, fake it till you make it. But now I'm telling you the truth, okay? I'm not happy. I can't sleep. I'm so angry it's insane. And I'm depressed. I cry every day.'

By this stage she was rolling out nuggets at a fast rate. At one point the judge had to ask her to slow down so the courtroom scribe could keep up. Speaking of when they encouraged her to go to rehab, Britney said, 'I don't even drink alcohol – I should drink alcohol, considering what they put my heart through.' She spoke bluntly of her conservators, saying, 'I don't owe these people anything – especially me, the one that has roofed and fed tons of people on tour on the road. It's embarrassing and demoralizing what I've been through.'

Then she put into words with heartbreaking simplicity what she dreamt and hoped of for her life: 'All I want is to own my money, for this to end, and my boyfriend to drive me in his f**king car.'

More specifically and objectively, she laid out her hopes in more legal terms. 'I've done a lot of research, ma'am,' she said, using that cute, respectful term she had grown up with. 'And there's a lot of judges who do end conservatorships for people without them having to be evaluated all the time. The only times they don't is if a concerned family member says something's wrong with this person.'

Here, Britney sniffed a potential obstacle to what she wanted: 'And considering my family has lived off my conservatorship for thirteen years, I won't be surprised if one of them has something to say going forward, and say, "We don't think this should end, we have to help her." Especially if I get my fair turn exposing what they did to me.' The guardianship had made her sceptical of those behind it, and understandably so. Explaining why she didn't want to see more therapists and psychiatrists, she broke hearts across the globe when she said, 'I'm scared of people' and added, 'It's not okay to force me to do anything I don't want to do.' These were raw, harrowing words.

Then, she turned to her claim that she had been prevented from becoming pregnant again. 'I would like to progressively move forward and I want to have the real deal. I want to be able to get married and have a baby,' she said. 'I was told right now in the conservatorship, I'm not able to get married or have a baby, I have [an IUD] inside of myself right now so I don't get pregnant. I wanted to take the [IUD] out so I could start trying to have another baby. But this so-called team won't let me go to the doctor to take it out because they don't want me to have children – any more children.'

Despite previous reports that she only wanted her father removed from the conservatorship, Britney told Los Angeles County Superior Court Judge Brenda Penny: 'It's my wish and my dream for all of this to end.' At the close of this harrowing testimony, the judge told Britney: 'I just want to tell you that I certainly am sensitive to everything that you said and how you're feeling and I know that it took a lot of courage for you to say everything you have to say today, and I want to let you know that the court does appreciate your coming on the line and sharing how you're feeling.'

The public and journalists, too, reacted with sympathy for Britney. She had been around for so long that many people had taken her to their hearts and hated to hear the testimony. Adam White of the *Independent* noted that he had been at a show in London that Britney had testified she felt forced into. 'When I heard Spears's words on that courtroom live stream, my mind immediately went back to the O2,' he said. 'Thousands had been crammed into the arena, singing along to hits and waving glowsticks. Few of us asked the questions we probably should have been asking.'

Stars and friends also spoke out, including Justin Timberlake. 'After what we saw today, we should all be supporting Britney at this time,' he wrote on Twitter. 'Regardless of our past, good and bad, and no matter how long ago it was ... what's happening to her is just not right. No woman should ever be restricted from making decisions about her own body.'

Madonna uploaded a photo of herself wearing a T-shirt with Spears' name on it and added a caption, stating, 'Give this woman her life back. Death to the greedy patriarchy that has been doing this to women for centuries ... Britney we coming to get you out of jail!' Meanwhile, her purported long-time rival Christina Aguilera tweeted, 'These past few days I've been thinking about Britney and everything she is going through. It is unacceptable that any woman, or human, wanting to be in control of their own destiny might not be allowed to live life as they wish.' Ariana Grande left a comment on Britney's Instagram: 'You are so very loved and supported,' the singer wrote.

The sands were indeed beginning to shift. A week later, and in light of Britney's colourful testimony, the wealth management company Bessemer Trust bowed out of the arrangement. 'Petitioner has become aware that the conservatee objects to the continuance of her conservatorship and desires to terminate the conservatorship,' a court filing stated. 'Petitioner has heard the conservatee and respects her wishes.'

There was a major blow for Jamie's case when *The New York Times* reported confidential new documents suggesting Britney's father had such control over her life that he even had the final say over what colour cabinets she had in her kitchen. The report revealed that although Britney had been publicly silent over the arrangement, behind the scenes she had been speaking out. As far back as 2016, she had complained to a court investigator that she was 'sick of being taken advantage of' and felt she was 'the one working and earning her money but everyone around her is on her payroll', the report said.

The same year, she had also informed the investigator that she wanted the conservatorship terminated altogether, reportedly stating that her father was 'obsessed' with controlling her life. 'She articulated she feels the conservatorship has become an oppressive and controlling tool against her,' the investigator wrote, adding that Britney said, 'Too much control ... Too, too much!' The *New York*

Times article also cited documents which stated that Britney had issues with her dad as far back as a hearing in 2014, noting his drinking and a 'shopping list' of other grievances. *The NYT* reported that she had been trying to end the conservatorship since at least the mid-2010s. These were bombshell revelations at just the moment Britney needed them most.

The details of the reports drove a wall though Jamie's previous suggestion that there was nothing to stop Britney ending the guardianship. 'Any time Britney wants to end her conservatorship, she can ask her lawyer to file a petition to terminate it; she has always had this right but in thirteen years has never exercised it,' Jamie's lawyer, Vivian Lee Thoreen, had told *People.* 'Britney knows that her Daddy loves her, and that he will be there for her whenever and if she needs him, just as he always has been – conservatorship or not.'

However, public opinion remained almost entirely on Britney's side. The case was becoming a hot topic. Perhaps inevitably, cynicism in some corners began to morph into almost conspiratorial territory. Some commentators began to speculate that the conservatorship was being drawn out with the agreement of all sides, to keep Britney relevant at a time when most of her contemporary stars were long forgotten.

But it was hard for anyone who had heard Britney's testimony to believe that she was a willing participant in any such purported theory. That statement had shaken everyone who had heard it. Even Jamie's lawyer, speaking on her father's behalf in court, said so. 'He is sorry to see his daughter suffering and in so much pain,' he said.

Chapter Eleven

IT'S UP TO HER

During 2021, as the Covid pandemic wore on longer than anyone hoped, it seemed to be a time of reckoning for some in the pop industry. Awareness of Britney's plight was soaring, and with it pressure mounted for her to be liberated. Meanwhile, other rumblings were growing. In the UK, a number of former *X Factor* contestants began to speak up about how badly they felt they were treated by the show. Rebecca Ferguson, Jedward, Lloyd Daniels and Cher Lloyd were just some of those who spoke out. Ferguson went as far as demanding a parliamentary inquiry into the controlling and bullying ways of the UK pop industry. Across the pond, US music bosses trembled as they feared a similar uprising from their stars.

The pressure for justice for Britney built further. Light appeared at the end of the tunnel in July 2021, when Judge Penny gave Britney permission to choose her own attorney in what was deemed a major victory for her. Former federal prosecutor Mathew Rosengart was named her new lawyer; it was good she had a strong advocate on her side, but the symbolism of the move was what counted most. A source told Page Six that Rosengart had 'multiple conversations' with Britney, adding, 'He has been keeping close tabs on her case for a while now and felt that her testimony last month was very compelling.'

He started with a bang, calling for an extensive re-examination of the entire arrangement and pushing for Jamie's immediate suspension as estate conservator. Then, in August, when Jamie agreed to step down as conservator 'when the time is right', the end was in sight. The paperwork stated that he 'intends to work with the court and his daughter's new attorney to prepare for an orderly transition to a new conservator'. This was not the final victory she was determined to fulfil, but it was her biggest step to date. It was not the end, but it was the beginning of the end.

In September 2021, Jamie's legal team filed a petition in the Los Angeles Superior Court to step down as conservator. In the legal paperwork, he referred to Britney's 'impassioned plea' to the court in two separate instances in June and July to terminate the thirteen-year-long conservatorship. 'As Mr Spears has said again and again, all he wants is what is best for his daughter,' the document said. 'If Ms Spears wants to terminate the conservatorship and believes that she can handle her own life, Mr Spears believes that she should get that chance.'

However, in a statement to the *Independent*, Britney's lawyer took a less conciliatory, far more cynical, view of this development. Rosengart said, 'Having exposed his misconduct and improper plan to hold his daughter hostage by trying to extract a multi-million-dollar settlement, Mr Spears has now effectively surrendered.'

He called Jamie's change of heart 'a massive legal victory'

for his mega-star client but pointed out that his team's 'investigation into financial mismanagement and other issues will continue'. He speculated that 'Mr Spears believes he can try to avoid accountability and justice, including sitting for a sworn deposition and answering other discovery under oath'. But, the lawyer added, 'as we assess his filing – which was inappropriately sent to the media before it was served on counsel – we will also continue to explore all options'.

On 29 September 2021, Jamie was officially suspended from Britney's conservatorship. 'The current situation is untenable,' Judge Penny said after hearing arguments from both Jamie's and Britney's attorneys. Alluding, perhaps unwittingly, to one of Britney's biggest hits, the judge added that the guardianship 'reflects a toxic environment'.

Meanwhile, the uncomfortable revelations kept coming. A follow-up documentary to *Framing Britney Spears*, titled *Controlling Britney Spears*, was released, containing several new allegations, including that Jamie placed surveillance equipment in Britney's room to listen to her conversations. It also alleged that he had access to her calls and messages. Britney's lawyer accused Jamie of 'horrifying and unconscionable invasions of his adult daughter's privacy' and called for his immediate removal from her conservatorship. However, Jamie's lawyer said Britney or a representative for her had been aware of the recordings.

A certified public accountant, John Zabel, was appointed temporary conservator of Britney's $60 million estate, in accordance with Britney's request. Jodi Montgomery remained temporary conservator of the person. But the moment Britney had waited so long for came in November, when Judge Penny ruled in favour of the singer's request to end the conservatorship altogether, a request which was not opposed by any of the parties involved. 'The court finds and determines that the conservatorship of the person and the estate of Britney Jean Spears is no longer required,' the judge said during an afternoon hearing. The judge added that further psychological assessments of Britney were unnecessary, because the conservatorship was technically voluntary. However, Judge Penny would continue working to settle ongoing financial concerns related to the case.

An expert told *The New York Times* she was surprised that the mandate was ended without a psychological assessment of Britney. 'Based upon the information on the public record, and the history of alleged mental health issues, I am shocked that the conservatorship was terminated without a current mental health evaluation,' said Victoria J. Haneman, a trusts and estates law professor at Creighton University. 'I had no doubt that a clear path to termination would be agreed upon, but I did not think in a million years that it would all end today.'

Although Britney was not present in court for the verdict, she had been spotted online ahead of the hearing. In a video posted to Instagram by her fiancé, Sam Asghari, she was wearing a T-shirt that read #FREEBRITNEY above the phrase, 'It's a human rights movement', while her track 'Work Bitch' played in the background. 'This week is gonna be very interesting for me!' she had written in a post. 'I haven't prayed for something more in my life!'

The news of her freedom caused excitement and hope for Britney and her supporters. Paris Hilton wrote on Twitter: 'I'm so happy to hear this news. It's been so long overdue, but I'm so glad that Britney is on her way to finally being free. Sending so much love!'

Celebrating the news on her Instagram account, Britney described it as 'the best day ever'. She told her 35 million followers: 'I think I'm gonna cry.' She added, 'Best day ever ... praise the Lord ... can I get an Amen????', with the hashtag #FreedBritney. She also took to Twitter, paying tribute to the campaigners who had worked so hard for her. '#FreeBritney movement ... I have no words ... because of you guys and your constant resilience in freeing me from my conservatorship ... my life is now in that direction!!!!!' she wrote. Asghari also posted his thoughts on Instagram. 'History was made today. Britney is Free!' he wrote, sharing an image displaying the word 'FREEDOM'.

Britney's fans outside the court were ecstatic. Jason Rivera, thirty-one, of Connecticut, waved a 'FREE BRITNEY' flag. 'It was overwhelming ... It was a sea of screams and cries,' he said of the crowd's reaction to the news. 'It almost felt surreal.' He added, 'I'm not a public crier, so I was choking back tears. It was so awesome to be a part of something bigger than yourself.'

Joshua Duran, twenty-nine, from California, came to the celebration rally with his fifty-one-year-old mother and called the court's decision 'a huge stress off everyone's back'. Added Duran: 'You could hear it in the crowd ... Everyone was screaming for joy. It's a huge victory for Britney, and it's a huge victory for everyone else who are in conservatorships as well.'

Speaking to the crowd outside the court, Britney's lawyer, Mathew Rosengart, said, 'This conservatorship was corrupted by James P. Spears. James P. Spears, as we all know, from public records ... took anywhere from $3 to $4 million from the estate. He took a salary from the estate. He took a percentage of his daughter's earnings from Las Vegas and otherwise.' The lawyer also praised the singer's 'courage' during the court hearings. He said he was proud that she had shone 'a light on conservatorships from California to New York' and noted that as a result of her testimony and campaign new laws had been passed 'to try to ensure that conservatorships like this ... do not happen again'.

To that end, the awareness of the issue prompted by Britney's case has already influenced a potential law change in the US. In 2021, the US House of Representatives was presented with a proposed Bill known as the FREE Act – Freedom and Right to Emancipate from Exploitation. The Bill said it 'would allow a person bound by a conservatorship to petition to replace their court-appointed private conservator with a public conservator, family member or private agent without having to prove abuse'.

One of the lawmakers who proposed the Bill said, 'Abusive conservatorships can be an unending nightmare, and tragically we don't know how many people are being held captive against their will under the broken guardianship system.' However, as Jennifer Otter Bickerdike revealed in *Being Britney*, many in the #FreeBritney movement opposed this planned law. It was felt that it would merely lead to a flood of professional conservators but do nothing to prevent the initial establishment of such abusive arrangements.

Rosengart was asked outside the court whether Britney would ever perform again. In a symbolic response, the lawyer said that, for the first time in years, 'it's up to her'.

Chapter Twelve

A NEW START

When Sam Asghari wanted to propose to Britney, he kept his plan largely secret. He asked his sisters and a friend to help him choose the ring, but otherwise he kept his plan to himself. 'I figured with her taste, she wouldn't want something super big and super celebrity,' he said. 'Celebrities get that million-dollar ring. And usually, it's free because it's for promotion, but I want it to represent something. I want it to come from my heart and I want it to go to someone that wasn't a big jeweller. It was a big company but it was a company that was willing to do it the way that I wanted it.' He described the engagement band as 'a really beautiful ring', 'a princess cut, for a real-life princess'.

He had 'Lioness' engraved on the inside of the ring. 'It came to me because I always figured the lion is lazy. The male lion has always been the symbol of the king of the jungle,' he said. 'But it's not true, it's really the female and she's very strong and she was very independent. And lioness was a beautiful name that just came to me out of nowhere.' Having sought out advice for the ring, he kept the rest of the experience private. 'I didn't tell anybody to be honest with you,' he says. 'I didn't want anybody to know and anybody to interfere in any way whatsoever so it was between me and her.' He proposed at their home. 'We do have videos of it but that's only for our eyes,' he said. Britney was surprised when he popped the question; she thought he was getting her a puppy.

Then Asghari took to social media, seemingly to confirm that the couple planned to wed. 'Our lives [have] been a real-life fairytale,' he captioned a photo showing the couple kissing, with Britney holding up her ring finger to present her engagement ring at the centre of the image. 'Happy Mother's Day to you my soon to be queen.'

Britney also announced a symbolic liberation from her conservatorship in April 2022, when she revealed she was expecting a baby. She shared a post on Instagram, saying she had taken a pregnancy test after Asghari had teased her about being 'food pregnant'. Having previously shared that she 'wants a family' with her partner, she wrote, 'I lost so much weight to go on my Maui trip only to gain it back … I thought "Geez … what happened to my stomach???" My husband said "No you're food pregnant silly!" So I got a pregnancy test … and uhhhhh well … I am having a baby… four days later I got a little more food pregnant. It's growing!!!'

She recalled the challenges she faced in a previous pregnancy, continuing, 'It's hard because when I was pregnant I had perinatal depression … I have to say it is absolutely horrible … Women didn't talk about it back then … Some people considered it dangerous if a woman complained like that with a baby inside her … But now women talk about it everyday … thank Jesus we don't have to keep that pain a reserved proper secret.' She concluded on a more hopeful note, saying, 'This time I will be doing yoga every day!!! Spreading lots of joy and love!!!' That said, Britney was not without trepidation regarding her impending motherhood. Writing on Instagram a week after her announcement, she returned to tell fans that she was 'scared to have a baby in this world, especially in America'.

Kevin Federline was quick to offer his best wishes, albeit via a lawyer's statement. 'Kevin is aware of Britney's Instagram post,' it read. 'He wishes her the best for a happy, healthy pregnancy and congratulates her and Sam Asghari as they plan for the excitement of parenthood together.' The following day, Britney showed off her 'small belly' in another post: 'I actually do have a small belly here but at least my pants fit ... Well barely!!! Psss is anyone curious why I'm four sizes smaller by the door???' she wrote.

Speaking to *Access Daily*'s Mario Lopez, Asghari said he would leave revealing the gender of the baby in Britney's hands. 'That's up to her, I don't want to [know],' he said. 'That is something I want to wait for ... If it is a daughter, it is gonna be the most spoiled princess ever. If it's a son, it is going to be the toughest son ever.'

Within weeks, Britney had a new announcement – one that was less dramatic but still significant. 'I'm going on a social media hiatus for a little while!!!' she wrote on Instagram on 24 April. 'I send my love and God bless you all,' she added. Amusingly, she accompanied her message with a video of a baby lounging in a chair wearing heart-shaped sunglasses, a fluffy robe and pink rollers in their hair.

However, within weeks she was back and causing concern for some of her fans, who were soon pleading with her to stop uploading nude snaps of herself on Instagram. Within the space of five hours, she had uploaded a series of very similar images over three separate posts. She captioned the initial post: 'Photo dump of the last time I was in Mexico BEFORE there was a baby inside me … why the heck do I look ten years younger on vacation.' The same photo was posted six times in total, with the only difference being shading and proximity to the camera.

She was seen covering her breasts with her hands while she used a pink heart emoji to cover her private parts. One Instagram user wrote, 'We don't need to see this, and we don't need to see it five times in a different filter,' while another sounded a similar note, saying, 'Please have a little respect for yourself and your children.' Someone else wrote, 'What are you doing stop it,' with another adding, 'Oh no Britney don't do this.'

This relatively harmless drama served as a reminder that many of Britney's fans will always be extra protective towards her, after years of open vulnerability and the conservatorship led them to feel they needed to keep an eye out for the troubled star. In any case, a behavioural psychologist said this sort of behaviour is a common trait after coercive control finally ends. Jo Hemmings told Femail:

> Having been under coercive control, whether it's a partner or the conservatorship of a parent, people will often have one of two reactive behaviours.

Either they become reckless, almost over-embracing their new-found freedom and make up for 'lost time' or they find it difficult to shake off the feeling of being controlled and may lurch into another relationship where the perceived relative safety of being confined to a degree, is still there.

Close watchers of Britney's affairs, of which there are so many around the planet, were pleased to see her not follow this path and seem content.

However, the couple's next update was anything but happy: Britney said she has lost her 'miracle baby early in the pregnancy'. Posting on Instagram, she said she and Asghari 'perhaps' should have waited to announce she was expecting until they were 'further along'. She said she shared the news of the miscarriage 'with our deepest sadness'. The couple said, 'Our love for each other is our strength' and added that 'this is a devastating time for any parent'. Nevertheless, said the note, the couple would 'continue trying to expand our beautiful family'.

Britney was very active on Instagram as this stage. A few days later she posted that she was taking solace in music to gain 'insight and perspective' after the miscarriage. Alongside a video in which she could be seen dancing to Beyoncé's 'Halo', she wrote, 'I'm definitely going through something in my life at the moment … and music helps me so much just to gain insight and perspective.'

A montage of her Mexico trip saw a clip of her captivated by a young girl as she carried her and gave her a cute kiss, saying in the caption that she 'fell in love instantly' with the youngster. She also shared several bikini clips, as well as topless ones as she frolicked on the beach with her fiancé. There was also a post with a darker edge. In a black-and-white text post, she wrote, 'My father taught me to be nice first, because you can always be mean later, but once you've been mean to someone, they won't believe the nice anymore. So be nice, be nice, until it's time to stop being nice, then destroy them.'

Speaking later to GQ, Asghari took a less frantic, and more positive, spiritual take on the miscarriage. The interviewer pressed him to discuss what had happened by pointing out that this approach can help normalize a traumatic incident. 'Yeah, it's positive,' he said. 'We're positive about it. It's something that happens to a lot of people. And one beautiful thing that I heard was when the baby's ready, it'll come. So that was a beautiful thing somebody had said was, it's a common process and the female body is just so amazing, and just the human body in general is so beautiful that it heals itself. And that when the baby's ready it'll be the right time.'

The following month, concerned fans aired their fears after Britney reposted old content and questioned whether someone else was running her Instagram page. The singer shared photos of herself on the beach in Mexico in a blue bikini, but hawk-eyed followers noted she had already posted similar images the previous month.

The suspicions that all might not be well with her were only added to when former *NSYNC singer Lance Bass told Page Six that he did not believe she was entirely free of the conservatorship. He said he had been unable to get in touch with her since her conservatorship was terminated in November 2021. 'Not at all,' he said, adding that he had tried hard to reach out. 'It's just, you know, there's a wall around her,' he claimed. 'And for some reason, those people don't want her old friends involved with her life.'

Britney and Asghari finally made things official when they married on Thursday 9 June, in a ceremony at their secluded Thousand Oaks home in Los Angeles. It was billed as a dreamlike fairytale occasion and provides a happy ending to this book.

To plan their big day, the couple had hired celebrity event producer Jeffrey Best of Best Events. 'We really wanted to make this a small and beautiful moment with family and friends,' Britney told *Vogue*. 'We wanted warm and feminine colors.' Makeup artist Charlotte Tilbury commented on Britney's 'natural beauty' and 'big, brown eyes'. Her bridal jewellery weighed 62 carats and came from Stephanie Gottlieb, known as the jeweller to the stars. The pieces included round diamond and pear-shaped drop earrings, a heart-shaped diamond tennis necklace in white gold and an oval diamond tennis bracelet.

She wore a sleek, off-the-shoulder custom Versace dress with a leg-revealing slit up one side and a classic white veil with satin edging. Asghari also chose Versace for his sharp tuxedo. Britney has chosen a stack of two bands to pair with her engagement ring, and Asghari also had two platinum bands. They arrived in style. Waiting outside the couple's home, which was draped in pink and white roses for the occasion, was a white horse with gold hooves, pulling a carriage designed for the occasion. 'Britney walked herself down the aisle. She looked absolutely stunning in her main dress,' said a source on *Elle*. 'She cried happy tears at some moments … It ended up being the happiest night for Britney. She wanted a fairytale wedding and she got it. Britney looked stunning.'

The guest list was small but glittering, including Madonna, Selena Gomez, Drew Barrymore, Kathy Hilton, Maria Menounos, Ansel Elgort, will.i.am, Britney's manager Cade Hudson and Donatella Versace. Paris Hilton had turned down an invitation to DJ for the US President to be there, having been asked to take to the turntables for Joe Biden's Summit of Americas dinner at the Getty Villa in Los Angeles.

The ceremony, which was just ten minutes long, took place under a tent draped in velvet blush. After the formalities, Britney wooed the guests at the party when she changed into no less than three more outfits, all by Versace. First, she wore a black mini-dress, then a two-toned outfit and finally a red mini-dress. The couple cut a vanilla strawberry cake.

Although there was no formal first dance, there was music, which was provided by DJ Albert. However, the musical highlights of the evening came when Selena Gomez, Madonna and Britney danced together to her hit 'Toxic', followed by Paris Hilton and Britney singing the socialite's 'Stars Are Blind'. The atmosphere remained jolly. At one point, Britney and Madonna recreated their famous MTV awards kiss. Britney later revealed that she had been wearing a diamond thong as she danced. With the celebrations finished, the newly-weds made a triumphant exit at 10.15 p.m. in a Rolls-Royce. As they drove away, their guests surrounded their car with sparklers.

Asghari's representative, Brandon Cohen, confirmed the couple's nuptials to the media, saying, 'I am very ecstatic this day has come, and they are married. I know he wanted this for so long. He is so caring and supportive every step of the way.' Then Britney took to Instagram to share her joy with her fans. She wrote that she was 'still in shock' and added, 'Fairytales are real' in a series of posts. She continued, 'WE DID IT!!! WE GOT MARRIED!! Gggggeeeeezzzzz!!!' Britney gushed that 'the ceremony was a dream and the party was even better!!!', adding, 'So many incredible people came to our wedding and I'm still in shock.'

Her parents and sister Jamie Lynn were not present, according to reports, as the conservatorship battle continued to cast a shadow over the family's relations. However, Jamie Lynn showed her support by liking the series of shots. Lynne also gave the occasion her approval in a comment on one of Britney's online posts. Commenting on a wedding post that included a photo of the singer and Asghari kissing on a balcony, her mother wrote, 'You look radiant and so happy! Your wedding is the "dream" wedding!'

However, the wedding could have been more of a nightmare had Jason Alexander, Britney's Vegas husband, got his way. Broadcasting live on Instagram, he ran through hillside trails and scrapped with security guards at the star's Thousand Oaks mansion, as he screamed, 'I'm Jason Alexander! The first husband! I'm here to crash the wedding!'

He then gained entry to the wedding tent where the ceremony was to be held just hours later, shouting, 'She's my first wife, she's my only wife!' Eventually, he was wrestled to the ground before being charged with trespassing, vandalism and two counts of battery after his tussles with Britney's security guards. Shortly after, a source told Page Six: 'Britney is shaken but doesn't want to let this get her down. Everyone is thankfully safe, and Jason is no longer on the property.'

However, she was not in a mood to forgive and forget, as her attorney explained to Page Six. 'Fortunately, Alexander is incarcerated and under an emergency protective order,' Matthew Rosengart said. 'I want to thank Sergeant Cyrus Zadeh, Detective Ken Michaelson and the Ventura County Sheriff's Office for their prompt and good work and look forward to working with law enforcement to ensure Alexander is aggressively prosecuted and hopefully convicted, as he should be.'

According to a copy of the order obtained by Page Six, Alexander had 'continuously trespassed' on Britney's property and 'had been advised that he was not welcomed'. The website also reported that the order claimed Alexander had a knife when he was arrested. When he appeared in court, Alexander pleaded not guilty to the charges. At the time of his arrest, authorities also learned that Alexander was wanted on a felony theft arrest warrant in Napa County, said CNN.

In some ways, the wedding is Britney's story in microcosm: she just wanted to make her dream come true, but she found that the success came with a price. Jason Alexander's intrusion into her dream day can be seen as a metaphor for anything from the paparazzi to the prurient obsession so many took in her from a tender age.

The conservatorship was represented on the day by those who were not there – her family. Its legacy will not lift for a while. In June 2022, *Entertainment Tonight* reported on court documents suggesting that Jamie was trying to compel his daughter to sit for a deposition. The paperwork claimed Britney was dodging the testimony and that she had signed a $15 million book deal to write a memoir about the very things she was refusing to speak of in court.

Referencing her Instagram posts, Jamie's legal team said, 'That Britney can speak about the very issues she publicly raises (including to cash a $15 million cheque) but suddenly would be "unduly burdened" by the litigation her counsel initiated is ridiculous.' As for her mother, she has tried to be more conciliatory, despite bad blood between the pair. Asked by reporters how she was feeling after not getting invited to her estranged daughter's wedding to Asghari, she said, 'I just want her to be happy.'

Inevitably, any reconciliation will be a complex affair. In July 2022, Britney accused her mother of helping to plot her conservatorship and hiding coffee from her. 'You abused me,' wrote Britney on Instagram. Her outburst came after Lynne had defended herself against criticism that she never texted her daughter back while she was in a mental health facility in 2019. Lynne had insisted that Britney did not share the 'whole conversation'.

Fans will await Britney's memoir with bated breath, but the longer they wait the more it suggests the star is, at last, in control. Rather than being at the behest of a merciless, money-making project which rushes from payday to payday, she is able to breathe and consider her next steps.

Having been featured in a newspaper at eight weeks old, taking dance classes at two and performing her first concert at four, Britney was in a rush from the start. Then, before she knew it, others had their feet on the pedals, and they would determine how fast she travelled. Naturally, her fans await new material and tours from their hero. But those with her very best interests at heart will also take joy from any intervening quiet time, because now, as her lawyer said outside the court when her conservatorship was finally lifted, it's all up to her.

ACKNOWLEDGEMENTS

Thanks to all of the marvellous team at Michael O'Mara Books, especially my editor, Lucy Stewardson, who was a joy to work with; Natasha Le Coultre, who designed a fabulous jacket; picture researcher Judith Palmer; typesetter Simon Buchanan; proofreader Rowena Anketell, who shares a birthday with Britney; and not forgetting LMD.

BIBLIOGRAPHY

Tom Bower, *Sweet Revenge: The Intimate Life of Simon Cowell* (London: Faber & Faber, 2012)

Steve Dennis, *Britney, Inside the Dream: The Biography* (London: HarperCollins, 2009)

Chas Newkey-Burden, *Simon Cowell: The Unauthorized Biography* (London: Michael O'Mara, 2009)

Jennifer Otter Bickerdike, *Being Britney: Pieces of a Modern Icon* (London: Nine Eight Books, 2021)

John Seabrook, *The Song Machine: How to Make a Hit* (London: Vintage, 2016)

Sean Smith, *Britney: The Unauthorized Biography* (London: Pan, 2005)

Britney Spears and Lynn Spears, *Heart to Heart* (New York City: Three Rivers, 2000)

Jamie Lynn Spears, *Things I Should Have Said* (New York City: Worthy Books, 2022)

Lynne Spears, *Through the Storm: A Real Story of Fame and Family in a Tabloid World* (Nashville: Thomas Nelson, 2008)

DISCOGRAPHY

ALBUMS

... Baby One More Time (Jive, 1999)
Oops! ... I Did It Again (Jive, 2000)
Britney (Jive, 2001)
In the Zone (Jive, 2003)
Blackout (Jive, 2007)
Circus (Jive, 2008)
Femme Fatale (Jive, 2011)
Britney Jean (RCA, 2013)
Glory (RCA, 2016)

SINGLES

'... Baby One More Time' (Jive, 1998)
'Sometimes' (Jive, 1999)
'(You Drive Me) Crazy' (Jive, 1999)
'Born to Make You Happy' (Jive, 1999)
'From the Bottom of My Broken Heart' (Jive, 1999)
'Oops! ... I Did It Again' (Jive, 2000)
'Lucky' (Jive, 2000)
'Stronger' (Jive, 2000)
'Don't Let Me Be the Last to Know' (Jive, 2001)
'I'm a Slave 4 U' (Jive, 2001)
'Overprotected' (Jive, 2002)
'I'm Not a Girl, Not Yet a Woman' (Jive, 2002)
'I Love Rock 'n' Roll' (Jive, 2002)

'Boys' (Jive, 2002)

'Anticipating' (Jive, 2002)

'Me Against the Music' (Jive, 2003)

'Toxic' (Jive, 2004)

'Everytime' (Jive, 2004)

'Outrageous' (Jive, 2004)

'My Prerogative' (Jive, 2004)

'Do Somethin'' (Jive, 2005)

'Someday (I Will Understand)' (Jive, 2005)

'Gimme More' (Jive, 2007)

'Piece of Me' (Jive, 2007)

'Break the Ice' (Jive, 2008)

'Womanizer' (Jive 2008)

'Circus' (Jive, 2008)

'If U Seek Amy' (Jive, 2009)

'Radar' (Jive, 2009)

'3' (Jive, 2009)

'Hold It Against Me' (Jive, 2011)

'Till the World Ends' (Jive, 2011)

'I Wanna Go' (Jive, 2011)

'Criminal' (Jive, 2011)

'Ooh La La' (Jive, 2013)

'Work Bitch' (RCA, 2013)

'Perfume' (RCA, 2013)

'Pretty Girls' (RCA, 2015)

'Make Me' (RCA, 2016)

'Slumber Party' (RCA, 2016)

'Mood Ring' (RCA, 2020)

'Swimming in the Stars' (RCA, 2020)

PICTURE CREDITS

Page 1: Everett Collection Inc/Alamy Stock Photo.

Page 2: Kevin Mazur/WireImage/Getty Images (top); Retro AdArchives/Alamy Stock Photo (centre); Terry Renna/AP/ Shutterstock (bottom).

Page 3: Kevin Mazur Archive 1/WireImage/Getty Images (top); Barry King/Getty Images (bottom).

Page 4: Reuters/Alamy Stock Photo (top); Everett Collection Inc/Alamy Stock Photo (centre); Entertainment Pictures/Alamy Stock Photo (bottom).

Page 5: Frank Micelotta/ImageDirect/Getty Images (top); Kevin Mazur/WireImage/GettyImages (bottom).

Page 6: MB Pictures/Shutterstock (top); *New York Daily News*/Getty Images (bottom).

Page 7: Kevin Mazur/Stringer/Getty Images for Jive Records (top); FOX Image Collection/Getty Images (centre); Kevork Djansezian/AP/Shutterstock (bottom).

Page 8: Marco Piraccini/Archivio Marco Piraccini/ Mondadori Portfolio/Getty Images (top); Kevin Winter/ Getty Images (centre); PictureLux/The Hollywood Archive/ Alamy Stock Photo (bottom).

INDEX